GRANDMOTHER EARTH XII:
2006

**Zebras, Zimbabwe at Hwange National Park,
Africa by AnneMarie Dyer**

GRANDMOTHER EARTH XII: 2006

Patricia Smith
Frances Brinkley Cowden
Editors

Marcelle Z. Nia
Mary Frances Broome
Editorial Assistants

Featuring
Award-winning
Poetry and Prose
from the

2005 GRANDMOTHER EARTH
NATIONAL WRITING CONTEST

GRANDMOTHER EARTH CREATIONS
Cordova, Tennessee

Cover Photo by Neal Hogenbirk (Cornelius)

His photography (as Neal Hogenbirk)
appeared in the first 12 volumes of *Grandmother
Earth* and often on the cover as in *Grandmother
Earth I.* In addition he had poetry or prose in
almost every volume. He also contributed freely
to many other publications of Grandmother Earth
and Life Press, most notably, *To Love a Whale*.

ISBN 1-884289-46-0   10.00

FIRST EDITION: 2006
GRANDMOTHER EARTH CREATIONS
P. O. Box 2018
Cordova, TN 38088
Phone: (901) 309-3692
gmoearth@aol.com
www.grandmotherearth.com

Cornelius Hogenbirk

This issue is dedicated to Cornelius Hogenbirk

"He was a loving, caring, gentle, generous brother, son and uncle." He served as a U.S. Army Signal Corps photographer in Japan during the occupation, covering the Yokohama war crimes trials. His first camera was a Brownie Hawkeye box camera, at age 10. His photography, articles, poems and prose have been published nationwide. He retired from Westinghouse and resided in Waretown, N.J. where he devoted his time to gardening and nature photography.

—his niece, AnneMarie Dyer

2005 GRANDMOTHER EARTH AWARDS

Judge: Madelyn Eastlund
Poetry Awards

1st Losing the Farm, Glenna Holloway, Naperville, IL

2nd Geese, June Owens, Zephyrhills, FL

3rd Cottonwoods, Kitty Yeager, Arkadelphia, AR

4th When the Moon Was Unreachable, Verna Lee Hinegardner, Hot Springs, AR

1HM Shiloh, Daniel Leonard, Oak Ridge, TN

2HM Standing in the Dark, Pat King, Albia, IA

3HM Carrying a Bucket of Stars, Rosalyn Ostler, Salt Lake City, UT

4HM The Art of Peace and Origami, Carol Ogdon Floyd, Linton, IN

5HM Hallelujah-kind-of-day, Rita Goodgame, Little Rock, AR

6HM Washday, 1920, Elizabeth Howard, Crossville, TN

Judge: Martha McNatt
General Prose

1st Eat Your Heart Out, Fred Astaire, Jo Anne Allen, Ola, AR

2nd A Neat and Tidy Crime, Phylis Warady, Grass Valley, CA

3rd Yellow Pages Romance, Carl Dana, Saratoga Springs, NY

HM The Washtub Adventure, John E. Clemons, La Crosse, WI

HM George, John E. Clemons, La Crosse, WI

Environmental Prose

1st Four Friends, an Improvisation, Marguerite Thoburn, Watkins, Lynchburg, VA

HM Through the Windowpane, Connie Spitter, Tucson, AZ

Judge: Pat Crocker
Humorous Poetry

1st Dentist's Nightmare, Gloria R. Milbrath, Port Dodge, IA

HM The Stripper, N. Colwell Snell, Salt Lake City, UT

Lost in the Bubble, 2055, Russell H. Strauss, Memphis, TN

Commitment, Michael R. Denington, Bartlett, TN

Humorous Prose

1st My Special Church Day, N. E. Chapman, Oklahoma City, OK

HM Aunt Zeenie's Almost New Shoes, Anne H. Norris, Memphis, TN

Yellow Pages Romance, Carl Dana, Saratoga Springs, NY

Wired for Flight, Meg Roman, Zephyrhills, FL

Judge: Lucile Ray
Short Form

1st Identity Crisis, Phylis Warady, Grass Valley, CA

HM A Poem I First Thought of in Memphis, Brett Taylor, Knoxville, TN

August by the Bay, Vincent Tomeo, Flushing, NY

United We Stand, Edna Carpenter Booker, Iowa, City, IA

Woodland Performance, Dena R. Gorrell,
Edmond, OK

Judge: Thomas McDaniel
Haiku

1st Sitting in silence, Frances W. Muir, Coral
Springs, FL

1HM One fern frond falls prey, Ellaraine Lockie,
SunnyDale, CA

HM Early Ozark Morning, Diane Stefan, Mountain
Home, AR
Senryu, Edna Carpenter Booker, Iowa, City, IA
Senryu, Michael R. Denington, Bartlett, TN
"Persnickety" pet, Annetta Talbot Beauchamp,
Helena, AR
Old mulberry tree, Meg Roman, Zephyrhills, FL

Judge: Marcelle Nia
Enviornmental Poetry

1st Solitude, Arla M. Clemmons, La Crosse, WI

1HM Losing the Farm, Glenna Holloway, Naperville,
IL

HM For Mississippi Blessing, Winifred Hamrick
Farrar, Meridian, MS
By Dawn's Early Light, Pame Bosman, Bunnell,
FL
Sweet Smells of June, Annetta Talbot
Beauchamp, Helena, AR
Wonderment of Dawn, Anne-Marie Legan,
Herrin, FL

Student Awards

1st Obsession, Courtney Watts, Ellicott City, MD
2nd The One, Christopher Watts, Ellicott City, MD
3rd A Bad Day, Cecilia Snow, Memphis, TN
4th Haiku, Cameron Hidayat, Memphis, TN

LOSING THE FARM

This shaggy hump of land
Comes down to settle at the shallow pond
Like our old dog, paws in his water dish.
The man I married was my father's only hand.
His first job was to stock the pond with fish.
Young Phil was smart. Why he would work for us
Was hard to understand.

He built a barn without
Much help that March my father hurt his hip.
Spring's greening nap resembled sheared chenille,
Our fields embroidered by the tractor's seeding route
Like Mama's bedspread pattern, Wheel-in-Wheel.
She died that June, then Phil was hired full time.
Sometimes he cleaned my trout.

I asked him how he knew
So much, and why he didn't take a job
With more to offer. Phil said he loved farming.
Before the corn grew ears he said he loved me too.
At first, my father found the thought alarming,
But soon he recognized his stroke of luck—
What blessings could accrue.

And so they did. The years
Were mostly kind, the rains and Phil were faithful.
He turned the scrub to terraces of grapes
Where domes of purpling autumn almost vanquish tears.
Now neighbors' spreads are gone, the city rapes
Its way toward us, my parents' hilltop graves,
And all our gravest fears.

Besides the pond, our lane—
The graveled last ditch lifeline left to drive
The truck to market, movies, church and vet—
Was just condemned--last ploy to make us sell. The pain
Of isolation's grip, our drought-grown debt
And kneeling crops conspire to push us out
Of our homemade domain.

With arteries now closed,
The heartbeat stops in this uneven Eden.
No mall, no high-tech electronics plant
Compares with tasseled corn, or beaded arbors posed
Against a moiré quilt in day's last slant.
Bulldozers quickly level secret places
Where the dying dog once dozed.

Glenna Holloway

COPPER KETTLE SWEETHEART

Some folks on the ridge thought Papa called Ma
his copper kettle sweetheart 'cause her hair
had both color and sheen of the dented
old kettle that Papa kept high-polished
and hung from a fat hook in the kitchen
and they laughed that Papa likened her so.
When ladies met for quilting they would tease
Ma and ask didn't she mind that Papa
called her that name instead of pretty words?
But Ma always answered she was suited.
My sister and seven brothers and me

sat beside Pa in the evening, like steps
on the porch—and we listened to him play
a lively tune on mouth harp or fiddle.
But mostly we liked best when he told tales
of when he was a boy. He'd point his pipe
up at the copper kettle. Ma would say
"Not again, Jeb, " but she'd poke her needle
pleased-like into her quilt block. I could see
by fire's glow her face flushed a pretty pink
He'd tell about the time he and his Pa
was sent into their cellar by his Ma
to bring up some potatoes for her stew.

"They was piled way back in a dark corner.
And darned if them spuds hadn't poked new roots
into the dirt floor. Sure a puzzlement!
Things don't grow in total dark. Then my pa
noticed the kettle Mama kept polished"
Our eyes went round oohs of surprise although
we knew the story well: how a slim beam
of afternoon sun came through the coal chute
"just about kissing the kettle." he'd say.
"That kettle just being there without plan,
-- that copper kettle so highly polished,
just couldn't help reflect the light that touched
right into that dark corner and the spuds
couldn't help be warmed and set down their roots.
He always ended, "We need a copper
kettle in our lives.-- don't never forget.
Your Ma, she's my shining copper kettle."

Madelyn Eastlund

The Lyric, **Spring, 2002**

SOLITUDE

Drifting down Rainy River
our canoe slips by pines
that fence ill the solitude
of the Lake of the Woods.

We see a painted turtle,
head withdrawn into its shell,
sleeping on a half-submerged log.
The splash of our paddles
does not intimidate.

We watch an egret
step warily on the bank
testing the waters for fish.
The bird knows he is being watched,
responds with a fluff of white plumes.

We pass a beaver's lodge.
No sign of occupants.
The air of the sphinx
surrounds this stretch of water
so we paddle faster.

We look back at the beaver's pyramid;
the blue-green water is calm
except for water bugs that circle
as if this is their Nile.

We return home to sip white wine,
taste whitefish, jicama, and mango,
steep ourselves in the last rays of sunlight.

We let our minds drift, lost in reverie,
until the wild laughter of a loon
rings across the star-dimpled lake
breaking our solitude.

Arla M. Clemons

IN MCDONALD'S PARKING LOT

the man sits on the station wagon's tailgate
playing his violin--oblivious
to ordinary happenings
around him. Pure notes

float like birds
through vacant air
before landing on hot concrete
between parked cars.

Is he on his way
to the regional violin—or is it fiddle—
retreat nearby? Unlike street comer performers
or subway musicians in big cities,

no crowds gather,
no applause, no money.
He plays folk songs on the instrument
same as heard in pioneers' homes.

Live dining music
as children clutch Happy Meal toys
and mothers' hands,
white-haired couples pause

in leisurely travel to no important destination,
workmen seek brief coolness for hurried meal.
Familiar sameness—that's why people stop
at golden arches. But today,

melodic spell unbroken as if commonplace,
no one questions why
a stranger shares music
in McDonald's parking lot.

Faye Williams Jones

DANCE OF DEATH

I wander down to the crystal green
pond and stare at the massive oak trees
surrounding the shifting waters,
casting dark shadows of jagged
black shapes on the ripples below.
Fallen leaves of color are struggling
with the wet silhouettes as if clinging
to the swaying branches above—
not yet willing to take a final *bow*
after their *Dance of Death.*

Jane E. Allen

HALLELUJAH-KIND OF DAY

In that dawn woodland, we drive through valleys
nestled in the foothills of the Smoky Mountains.
The forest belongs to us-- quiet, sacred as a chapel.
Sunlight streaks through phantom haze
to parade pine shadows across our path.
In a hollow, our pace quickens. Evergreen fragrance
mingles with drifting scents of country ham.
An early riser stokes his campfire. Maybe he is hungry, too.

In this pristine forest, a family of vocalists
sway in our Country Squire station wagon.
Open windows channel crisp mountain air into our lungs.
Ribboned hair tangles and flaps in buffeting gusts.
We begin to harmonize in Girl Scout rounds
choir chant "Glorias" and giddy made-up ditties,
belting out each allegro with rollicking
enthusiasm of an Opening Night.

On a bend, campers armed with firewood
stand, heads cocked, their eyes fixed upon our
fleeting ensemble until we are lost in a turn.
In the distance, a stretch of road reveals a family
gathered on the shoulder straining to see...us?
Lyrics bounce off grandfather mountain's rocky crest
while summer-tanned youths catch our song and run with it.

We pause in the spontaneity of the moment
and rejoice in the myriad of small pleasures.
Basking in a hallelujah-kind-of-day
we drive with sky in our eyes-- we soar without wings.

Rita L. Goodgame

STANDING ON THE PROMISES OF GOD

And lo a voice from heaven, saying, "This is my
beloved Son, in whom I am well pleased. "
                                    Matthew 3:17

I did not know how anyone could stand
on promises, but tossing back my head
I sang that song, and hoped for solid land
beneath my feet. At nine, there's lots to dread.

I knew I would not like the flames of hell
so I confessed my sins. They baptized me
in all three names. I thought, " A voice will tell
me I am loved; a dove, my legacy."

My Mama said she came up clean and pure.
I came up gasping, jerking like a hen
without a head, bone-wet—but I was sure
I heard that organ promising again;

and, as I sang along, dried off and dressed,
a gust of warmth assured me I was blessed.

Verna Lee Hinegardner

trumpet vine weaves
through honeysuckle announcing
ripe berries

Sandra O. Hancock

8

GEESE

you say this snowing river
is too deep for us to wade through
flows too fast for counting
that I am not able
to pull ashore alone

and *you* are not a safe little pond

for me to innertube

you say *you* opened my poems
on your firelight table
let the fire read them
let the embers remember words
and that the fragile shadows
in my orchards are only moon-wishes

that all the sun's lenses
have ever recorded or cared about
are small lifeless forms lying in my fields
between broken stems

that trees are really owls
drawing history into circles
of pitch where unsuspecting
spiders and ants and gnats are stuck

you say the sea
is an awful monster
who swallows the light
and spits it back
less light than it was

9

you may tell me all of this
that there is really nothing now
but birth and death
with only a brief pause to separate
and I will nod agreement
study blueness of my fingernails
want to say wait   listen   if
that is so why am I stunned
to silence   made full of
rapture by the light   the flashes
of light that burst between
the northward throbbing geese

June Owens

SHILOH

I walked along the sunken road of Shiloh,
looked over where had been the peach orchard;
its falling blossoms had resembled snow
to both union and confederate soldiers
as they fell upon the dead and dying
while the guns fired across the field.
Nearby was what they'd call the hornets' nest,
the buzzing mini balls swishing by heads.

Hearing a mourning dove, I felt the gentle breeze,
heard the wind rustle through the oaks behind me.
I walked around what's called bloody pond,
the pond once bloodied by wounded men
of both sides, many getting their last drink,
some while the battle still raged around them,
knowing their part in the battle was no more.

Oh, how I wondered how this place,
named from a Hebrew word that means
place of peace, was in fact the place of death
for oh so many, the most ever until that time.
How could it now feel so calm and peaceful?
And then I felt I knew. I knew it in a touch
of soothing warmth upon my shoulder,
and a sweetness in the air like angels breathing.

It was not the hate, not the killing,
not the rage, that left its tranquil mark here,
its forever lasting, unmistakable signature.

No, it was the fervent prayers on dying lips,
the prayers of forgiveness, the removing
of little testaments, of agreeing to hate no more,
of entering a new and everlasting Shiloh,
one that truly is indeed a place of peace.

Daniel Leonard

One fern frond falls prey
to aphid infestation
Another unfurls

Ellaraine Lockie

COTTONWOODS

With leaves like golden butterflies in flight,
When autumn breezes flutter every tree,
The cottonwoods are whispering tonight
Like ladies sharing gossip over tea.
As wind entangles vines of scuppernong
And swishes through the pines in mournful tones,
A crystal river plays a liquid song
Of shallow water rushing over stones.
The forest voices speak of other times,
When men in eagle feathers ruled the land.
I hear their ghostly drums, their bony chimes,
And find their arrowheads in river-sand.
When sorrows come in shadow-colored hoods,
I run to hear the wind in cottonwoods.

Kitty Yeager

WOODLAND PERFORMANCE
(Cinquain)

Golden
daffodils dance
along a greening trail...
Choreography: courtesy
spring wind.

Dena Gorrell

THE ART OF PEACE AND ORIGAMI

The paper crane of peace
needs no weapons,
does not need to be strong,
is not greedy and has no enemies.

How do we create peace?
No one seem to have the answer.
People say they want it,
they fight and kill for it,
but we do not have peace.

Without care, without weapons,
a child folds love into paper
and gives life to a bird.
A child has the art of peace.

We can learn the subtleties
of paper folding.
I will give you white paper
        and we can all make cranes.

Carol Ogdon Floyd

WHEN THE MOON WAS UNREACHABLE

When cars had running boards
and gravel roads led home,
I slipped through the years
like an otter through a stream.

Only the moment was important
and life was a dawn-to-dark project
steadied by two constants:
    Mama with her lilting laughter
    Daddy with his time-tested jokes.

    Life was a montage of movement:
    Mama sewing on her treadle Singer
    Daddy shelling seed corn in coal oil
    watching fireworks at Walton Park
    playing Go-Sheep-Go in the timber
    picking blackberries and gooseberries
    making ice cream Sunday afternoons
    Mama kneading dough; crocheting
    Daddy plowing unwilling fields
    playing pinochle, croquet, horseshoes
    running, jumping, teasing, giggling
    praying out-loud on my knees
    kissing and hugging
    always kissing and hugging

When wheat fields were golden
and raindrops were silver,
we circled the Philco on Saturday nights
and life moved forward
with no thought of beginnings or endings.

When the moon was unreachable,
my family was loyal as roots to flowers
angel-visited and angel-blessed.

Verna Lee Hinegardner

SWEET SMELLS OF JUNE

If I were struck
both blind and deaf today,
then I could live—
at least a thousand years—
on just the smells of June.
I could find a spot
tucked somewhere between
the pink-heavy air of a mimosa tree
and the sweet-green scent
of cottonwood.
   I'd have no need
   to hear the thunder
   or see the drops
   to prove the rain
   for I can smell a rain
   five miles away.
Great drops would splash
and lick the dust
from streets and lawns.
Hot concrete, cooled,
would send up steamy odors
and I could breathe the grass growing.

Annetta Talbot Beauchamp

STANDING IN THE DARK

Remember, Father, when I was a very little girl
and afraid of the dark
not because of bears and crocodiles
but because the sky was so wide
and I called you from the living room
golden with lamps   deep voices   light laughter
to save me from the hovering questions
that circled the ceiling above my bed:
but how can the sky go on forever?
and how many stars are there?
and if the sky's shaped like a doughnut
who's holding the doughnut?
And if we go to heaven when we die
how long will we live up there?
and what does forever mean?

And you, after long silence,
stroking my hair: I don 't know.
None of us know.
But your voice softened the dark
and I never knew when you left the room

In the years that followed when I left home
and you aged and weakened alone
were you afraid of the dark? I left the room
afraid to ask
before you closed your eyes.

What does it matter, now that you
are past the fear of fear?
It matters now for me:

must I stand in the dark alone?
No, because your grave's no tiny plot
but the whole green earth and the sea
and the whole wide sky
and they are still and always there
with answers—
most often: I don't know.
But memory ties time together
and again the darkness softens
as if you had never left the room.

Pat King

AUGUST BY THE BAY

August sky
Leaned over a moon
Ate the night

Crystallized bay cleaved giggled rippled folded
Like wrinkles on a satin sheet

Vincent J. Tomeo

CARRYING A BUCKET OF STARS

She thinks I walk on water, she thinks I hung the
moon.

Andy Griggs

They say beginning love glows sweet but spare
as spider webs in sun. I'd break that rule
and lift the spark for space to open, flare

into a wider filigree in air.
They tell me time can turn love cold or cruel,
they say beginning love, though sweet, can spare

but little of itself, but I would dare
to give it all and keep the fire well-fueled.
I'd make that spark an open flame, with flair

beyond my simple style, and freely bare
the passion I hold deep inside, a jewel
to burn a growing love more sweet. I'd spare

no bounty, even pull to earth the stars
to glitter in our eyes, and hope that you'll
ignite bare space and spark an open flare

of ecstasy the world would ever swear
was all that one could dream for, more than full
enough to make our love blaze sweet, yet spare
one flash to light the sky with dazzling flare.

Rosalyn Ostler

18

WASHDAY, 1920

A rare day to herself, older children in school,
babies with granny, Viney heads to the spring
at first light, skipping along dew-sprinkled
stones, in tune with wind stirring willows,
hundreds of birds singing. She dips water,

yokes wooden buckets across her shoulders,
her morning song muted already. She trudges
to the yard which needs sweeping, shoos hens
scratching holes under the crabapple. She
pours water in the kettle, sets kindling ablaze,

fetches more water. So much needed for a
household of six, diapers, overalls and dresses,
socks and underwear, sheets and towels.
Unending the dirt garnered from gardens,
fields, pastures. Even her plot of zinnias—red,

gold, yellow—so bold the sight of them flurries
her hands through kitchen chores. Tub full,
kettle nigh to boiling, she begins with the
whites, scrubs piece by piece on the rubboard,
wrings, rinses, wrings again. The suds make

rainbow beads in her arm hair, likely the only
beads she'll ever have, but for the cranberries
she wears to church. Her wrists ache, knuckles
red, one raw, stinging. She boils the whites in
the kettle of bluing, face bathed in steam and

hickory smoke, pokes up the fire, adds sticks.
Sweat rises on her neck in spite of the cold

wind. How she would like to rip off these
binding clothes and splash in the tub, or better
yet, in the branch where she'd once played.

In time, lines of clothes frolic about the house,
diapers and sheets doing the Virginia reel,
her man's underdrawers clogging, though they've not
danced since the wedding day. Even her faded
dresses shimmy shamelessly. She scrubs the

floors with dirty washwater, loosening refuse
her man has tracked from cow barn and pigsty .
She returns to the spring for more water—for
cooking and drinking. A thin stream ripples
down the rocks into a cauldron of light. Some

force she cannot name urges her to dip into
the icy kettle. She takes off her dress, her
underclothes, tosses them onto the rocks.
The torn fringes of her petticoat flutter like
white butterflies. She steps in gingerly,

stifling the need to shriek from the coldness.
The water swirls about her, bathing feet,
legs, loins, breasts. She rises, shivering, yet
serene. She cups her lustrous belly, a cave
swimming with new life, her secret for now.

Elizabeth Howard

DENTIST'S NIGHTMARE

They both complained, "My teeth don't fit."
They saw the dentist in a snit.
When the verdict came, oh, brother,
Each wore the dentures of the other!

Gloria R. Milbrath

COMMITMENT

this week I shall devote a day to poetry
—an entire day—

or at least the waking part of it
—the entire waking part—

after a Danish and espresso breakfast

or at least the afternoon
—the entire afternoon—

after a salad at Milano's

or at least the evening
—the entire evening—

after a glass of *eis wein*

21

yes, I shall devote the day

dredge a creative idea
from my pitch-black idea pit

develop it into verse
—deliver it to the *New Yorker*—

or at least the refrigerator door
—my refrigerator door—

yes, this week I shall devote Wednesday
to poetry—

but this is Thursday—

next week I shall devote a day to poetry
—an entire day—

Michael R. Denington

SENRYU

Children, lovers weep
at shining, black granite slabs—
Nation's healing wall

Michael R. Denington

LOST IN THE BUBBLE, 2055

Forgive me, dear. You do look cute
wearing your chic new bubble suit
of sheerest plastic, spun much finer
than silk by Jacques, the great designer,
whose infomercials now extol
styles with thermostat control.
In his bubbles, rain and snow
are never felt. When cold winds blow
he keeps your temperature quite right,
at just above seventy Fahrenheit.
My dear, in order to survive
the fashion scene in fifty-five,
the wearer must stand proud, aloof
in a suit that's bomb and bullet proof
with a subtle hood over face and hair
that purifies the city air.
Accessories? Your comfort zone
includes a pendant telephone.
A two-inch microchip computer
has made your outfit even cuter.
I do adore your look, those clothes
that cover you from toe to nose.
I love your purchase, dear, I swear,
but you're somewhere inside
and I must confide,
I don't know where.

Russell H. Strauss

UNITED WE STAND

Old King George The Third,
his future looking blurred,
caused a 'Revolutionary' fuss
but we decided...we must be U S.

Edna Carpenter Booker

sparkling canning jars
cherries, peaches, crabapples
found—all in a jam

Edna Carpenter Booker

HARVEST'S REWARD
Adelaide Crapsey Cinquain

Jammed jars
of peaches, beans,
and black-eyed peas form ranks
on shelves in cellar's coolness. Fall's
bounty.

Von S. Bourland

THE STRIPPER

She practically cooed
as she danced in the nude,
her smooth body flawless,
supple and bra-less.
She waltzed through the kitchen
with nary a stitch on,
her socks and her undies
and various sundries
lay stacked all the while
in a loose little pile,
my temperature rising
while she kept disguising
intents and demands
with her deft, charming hands.
The way she was acting
was kind of distracting,
intent, I am sure, on capturing me;
of course, she succeeded. She's only three.

N. Colwell Snell

Clematis lovely
Twining green and lavender
Majestic blossoms

LaVonne Schoneman

Moon over Deception Pass by David Millison

THAT "MOON THING"

Strange powers flow from moon's eerie glow—
All of creation seems to know.
Primitive man, intuitively attuned,
was able to commune with sun and moon.

26

Phases of the moon, in an erratic way,
waxes and wanes in confused disarray.
Moon hides for days—disappears—
comes back to life—reappears.
Hovers owl-like from the sky
spying on earth with one giant eye.
Associated with land-of-the-dead,
monsters, demons, fill aborigines with dread.
Evil spirits haunt moonless nights—
early man defends with rituals and rites.
Strange things happen during fitful moon-moods—
its capricious, volatile interludes.

Moon myths and legends that still exist
began eons ago in primordial mist.
Moon affects how crops grow—
tells farmers when to sow.
Even tides hear the moon—
sway to-and-fro to its tune.
Some folks become strange—
kind'a deranged.
Sad people become sadder;
bad people—badder.
Lovers act moony 'n spooney,
rest of us—a bit loony.
Dogs 'n wolves begin to howl—
cats prowl 'n yowl.
All animals are aware
when there's a full moon up there.

Devilish feelings awakening?
Blame 'em on that "moon-thing".

Marjorie Millison

MORNING SONGS

Cackle ye chickens
While ye may,
Old farmer's hands are prying,
And these new eggs
You've laid today
Tomorrow will be frying.

W. H. Holland, Jr.

"THERE IS A SEASON, SON. . ."

It was a different sight
seeing Mama lie there so still
in her staid nursing home room.

She had been a busy one in the past,
giving birth to ten children over twenty years,
nursing them, feeding them, clothing them,
caring for their souls as well.

Cooking meals alone for such a crew
had called for Wall Street timing.
But the long table with its red-checked oil cloth
and its two long wooden benches on each side
shone with heaping bowls of tasty dishes Southern
style:
smooth milk gravy, fluffy white biscuits,
and smokehouse sugar-cured ham.

In between the hours of child toil
she labored in the fields alongside Papa,
hoeing the peas and corn, picking the white cotton bolls
at fall harvest time.

The packed smokehouse glowed with Mason jars
of green beans, and red tomatoes,
with hanging hams from January hog kills
and rows and rows of sausage- filled glass.

Now she lay there on her antiseptic bed
still, quiet, her lips moving with slow speech,
reviewing past events of a mother's care,
sometimes with joy -- sometimes with fright
over danger waiting in the silent dark,
as bright red flowers mocking her busy life
stood tall and proud over her.

I held her hand and spoke soft words of joy
rejoicing in the life of one who gave so much—
one who cared—one who loved—one who shared,
recalling her soft words in times past to me:
"There is a season, son, for all things."

John W. Crawford

Night shifts to reveal
Cobweb threads in morning rays
Spider awaits prey.

CJ Clark

AFTER THE RAIN

We meet at the Union's Art Fair.
You buy me a painting
for thirty-five dollars
of a couple embracing under the moon.
 I say, "That girl is me."
You say, "1 think the gentleman is me."

It starts to rain so you wrap
the painting in your coat.
Tenderly, you cover it like a child.
 I cross the arms to tie it tight.

We run down the street,
splash in the puddles,
stick out our tongues to taste
the drops. We run into a man
with an open umbrella
who mutters, "Slow down."

We stop at Fayze's for coffee,
sit at a table with a checkered cloth,
hold hands like we are in love.
The waiter asks, "Is this an anniversary?"
I say, "Yes, four-weeks."
You say, "Since Valentine's Day."

The waiter returns, holding
a cupcake with four lighted candles.
We blow them out. Make a wish.
Blue smoke curls to form a question mark.

You walk me home, where we kiss
under the porch light.

Our bodies in the shadows
breathe as one.

You walk away, whistling. .
I watch until darkness steals you
before I open the door to go inside

This was the last time I saw you.
I heard you went back to your hometown,
met a girl from Ohio.

On rainy days, I still look at you
in the painting on my wall
holding me under the moon.

Arla M. Clemons

sitting in silence
          gong's ringing stirs the air—
                    ripples on water

Frances W. Muir

DADDY LONGLEGS

The harvestman
is waiting at the door
when I come calling.
This imposing creature,
endowed with many eyes,
does not move, as if to say,
"This spot is mine."
Hovering over the doorbell light,
he dares me to touch
the entrance to this home.
Confident
that he will
not retaliate
with barbs or stings,
I reach between
his straddled legs,
press the button
that unleashes
a symphony of song.
Resonating bells
do not disturb his reverie;
he remains steadfast.
This pompous daddy longlegs
continues to bask in the sun,
hoping a misguided insect
will join him for his brunch.

Arla M. Clemons

SISTERS

Marilla and Matilda are sisters
who live together in a cubicle
crowded with twin beds,
two walnut dressers, two wooden chairs,
a single desk.

A mirror hangs above Marilla's dresser.
Matilda avoids her reflection now
because her youthful beauty has faded.
Her grey hair and wrinkled skin
make her turn away.
Once Matilda wore long skirts,
provocative peasant blouses,
always wrapped herself in red.

Marilla is retired,
still wears her orthopedic shoes,
the tailored suit of the teacher.
Never a hair out of place,
never flamboyant—
always ordinary.

Sometimes Matilda dances
in the room, tosses her long hair,
swings her hips, closes her eyes
to reminisce.

Marilla sits straight in her chair.
Her dark-rimmed glasses scanning the page.
She folds her letter edge to edge,
prints her return address— Elridge Oaks
Nursing Home, Room 217.

When Matilda came to the nursing home,
she had a mirror above her dresser too.
One day, she waltzed up to the glass.
Puzzled by the stranger there,
she smashed the image with her brush
and threw her combs away.

Arla M. Clemons

CHOPPING KUDZU

In Georgia, the legend says that you must close your
windows at night to keep it out of the house.
from "Kudzu" by James Dickey

These vines reminded him
of his first wife, how she clung
tenaciously and would not let go,
claiming more and more space
until she choked all growth.
"Kudzu is alien and cunning
like a mail order bride, " he muttered,
"and she is choking the South."
He knew her history,
how Madame Kudzu was introduced
as an ornamental shrub at the Centennial Exposition,
how the Soil Conservation Service during the
        Depression
planted her for forage and erosion control,
how this Japanese femme fatale

with no American enemies
began to swallow soybean fields and pine forests.
Georgia, Mississippi, Alabama
became her homes, where she decorated
rusty John Deeres and corroding Chevrolets,
deserted barns and forlorn shacks
with frilly green carpeting.
"A thousand years from now," he reflected,
"every trace of our civilization
will be buried in the bosom of kudzu."
He began chopping again
where her lacy arms writhed up a telephone pole.
Swinging his machete, he reflected,
"I would never treat her like this
if she behaved like a lady."

Russell H. Strauss

SPIRIT GUIDE

I choose the mighty eagle
as my spirit guide
I see more clearly
through her telescopic eyes
The vision clearly focused
just before dawn
As nature and I meld into one.

Angela Logsdon

CHAIN POEM

Important! Read carefully!
Do not disregard
this message—It is real.
When you receive this poem,
open your mind.
Write down seven thoughts
expressed as mental pictures.
(These thoughts can be on any subject:
politics and sorrow, love
and sorrow, life and sorrow. . .)
Do not discard this poem
or terrible things will happen:
Ideas will be abandoned unexpressed,
love will not be spoken,
a concrete image will dissolve in tears.
A man in Alabama received this poem:
within twenty-four hours of reading it,
his blindness had been lifted.
A woman in New Jersey got this poem:
within one week of reading it, she began
a journal which clarified her life.
You, too, can use this poem
to your good fortune. Here is how:
Express an idea concisely and beautifully
as you can. Write a title at the top of the page.
At the bottom, sign your name preceded by
a small, circled "c" and the date.
Read it aloud to five of your best-loved friends.
Wait for results to follow.

Carol Clark Williams

HANNABERRY LAKE BAPTISM

Strong arms lift me
from the warm waters.
I rise, gasping for air—
my white robe clinging tissue-like
to my dark skin.
As I struggle toward the sounds
of hymns and shouts of "Hallelujah!"
I raise my arms to Heaven, crying, "I don' died once!
I ain't gon' *die* no mo!"
Water stirs around me;
I watch the waves carry my sins
to the opposite bank.

Annetta Talbot Beauchamp

THE GRASS IS GREENER

And the younger of them said to his Father,
'Father, give me the share of property
that falls to me. '   Luke 15: 12a

I asked; he gave—no questions.

~

Life played dull, dull, dull—
        no arena workouts
        no Sabbath competitions
        no theater privileges
                like the Sadducee boys.
And school—such a babble—
        all reciting Scriptures aloud.

Mother's piety lessons
        fell around my ears
        like aniseed
        to our earth-packed floor.
And why should I have to learn Greek?
        I wasn't looking to go
        into Father's business.
But when Mother read in the Law
        about sons' rights
        to their father's wealth,
        I perked up.
        One third? Today?
                ~

Now I can head down the coast,
        check out the beach,
        kibitz with the fish-picklers
        in Tarichiae.
No more hoeing wheat and flax
        alongSide my hot-tempered brother.

Good-bye, Mother. I'll write.

Patricia A. Laster

Moon rises behind
congregation of mountains
Marries stars to snow

Ellaraine Lockie

38

EARLY SPRING AT SARDIS LAKE

Awake to rawest dark: no stars, no moon.
A few faint lights reflect across the lake,
as imperceptibly the world is soon
transformed through shades of gray, the call of loon,
and slowly brightening sky to fresh daybreak.
Like pencil lines, the barren trees are drawn
against the sky, and then all nature wakes.
A pair of mallards shuffle on our lawn,
as honking geese fly toward the glowing dawn.
A golden eagle spears a trout and takes
it to a nearby tree, has brunch with us.
By noon a front blows through with hostile cold.
We hurried, packed our car and withdrew; thus
we beat the storm as spring was put on hold.

Patricia W. Smith

SENRYU

"Persnickety" pet
Snubs nose at pricey dog food—
Then licks cat's bowl clean.

Annetta Talbot Beauchamp

ENDURANCE

The burning sand and blazing sun
Had scorched the runners of Mesquite,
When over the mountains came the rumble
That dropped a deluge at its feet.
For days the sun had burned on end,
Sapping every drop within.
Never cooling, ever baking,
Ever burning, always taking,
Merciless and all-pervading,
No relenting, never failing. . .
Until the wind blew from the west,
Until the thunder tolled the test,
Which the parched land must survive,
If it were to abide. . . alive.
A low rumble - first, just there.
Then louder, booming, filled the air.
Came it then en masse crescendo
Then the harsh and sweetening wind-blow. . .
 Some well-rooted, well-entrenched,
Some too shallow, too loose, cinched.
The prime drop smashed the sand - exploded!
And steamed the runners' skin.
Another, then one more, unloaded
Again- Again - Again. . . ,
Until the void was overflowing,
Until the valley was full sealed.
Drowning every nook and crevice,
Pouring water. . . oh, surreal. . .
Through the days of long recession,
Bits of Mesquite could be seen,
Swirling down the gushing arroyos,
But the runners, sleek and lean,
Were the last to show their faces,

As the water left high places.
There among the mud of summer
Stood the simple Mesquite runners;
Stood - Survived - and Flowered, aching,
Stored the excess for the days,
For the time of burning, baking,
Time of want and desolation;
Stood its ground, maintained its station,
Bracing for the next assaulting,
Seeing God, and . . . exalting.

William B. Caudle, II

FOR MISSISSIPPI BLESSING

I must go home to Mississippi hills
When rich October comes with azure skies
And fills the hollows with her lilac spills,
Her hints of amethyst and purple dyes.
I need to walk along untended ways
Through feathered grass turned copper-pink and gold,
Through daisies and wild asters caught in praise
Of something I would reach and firmly hold,
The same bronze peace that waits on polished leaves
When they lie fallen on their winter bed,
Their flaming splendor blown on wind that grieves
Their passing vibrant days, their glory fled.
But who would doubt serenity expressed
By ash-blue hills declaring we are blessed. .

Winifred Hamrick Farrar

ON MOON WINGS

You left a million heartbreaks ago today
and I stand at my midnight window
while last year's slow moon
ghosts your image to my eyes…
your breath to my breathing…
squeezing freezing that moment
of your existence into extremities not yet
discovered
into spring-colored canyons of time,
and the sound of your laughter
is a waterfall, washing me silver—silent…
the beat of you deeper than pain
sharper than scent of roses after rain.

I code you into my memory book…
your journey is complete…
your sandals still like moon wings on your feet.

But the moon wanes…
The moment vanishes
back into the night
from which it came.
I wonder if the angels
know your name.

Frieda Beasley Dorris

RIVER WANTS

Listen to the river
Speak to the stones.

Touching
Heats
Stones.

They know things
That touch our wanting—
 It's the reason we are here
Listening to the river
Speak with the stones.

Thoughts river deep
Want to be known
To feel
Fresh broken stones.

Reach into the bed where they lay
Supporting the river,
Growing wiser.

Stones
Cool the thighs
Of our wanting.

Peace—
Be still.

Carrie Inman

Photo by Jane E. Allen

LITERARY JUSTICE

The majestic courthouse
once kept secrets of true guilt and
innocence within its vast brick walls...
whispering to the wind of murders,
beatings, rapes, and thefts.
The peaceful old courthouse

now displays memorabilia of
To Kill a Mockingbird...
whispering to the wind of reflection,
enjoyment, and pride.

Literary justice.

Jane E. Allen

(Note: Hurricane Ivan showed its fury in Monroeville by lashing out at the famous courthouse in September, 2004. Fortunately, a movie company with special equipment was in town, and they quickly boarded up the windows, preventing the high winds from damaging this historical site.)

Photograph by Neal Hogenbirk

45

AFRICA'S BALLET

Ballet of a breeze
moving weightless
cloudlike canopies
of shimmering leaves,
where red and gold finches
and brilliant kingfishes
whirl their dervish dances
in their courting
plumage of spring.
The graceful rhythm of giraffes
as they canter through the veldt,
their long-stretched necks swaying
like the masts of fishing boats
in a swell.
Zebras stand shy and halting,
as they raise their magnificent
velvet-smooth heads,
neighing before they step into
their striped jeweled reflections
mirrored in the pool.
A pair of ostriches join them,

strutting ludicrously through the rustle

of weeds with a fine parade of bustles.

As the day begins to fade,
a soaring Pegasus Flight of leaping impala
move through swirls of copper light.

This remembrance sweeps past my mind's eye
as I gaze at the photos upon my wall,
where a sun-braided land walks hand in hand
with intricate dance and song.

Anne-Marie Legan

I MISS THE COWS

The meadow where the Black Angus
walked on all fours and fed freely
have gone from the valley.
They were directly across the river
from my porch.

How I miss them not being here
on the scene. They belonged
and fit wonderfully well
with the dirt road, butterfly weed
the Queen Anne's lace, and dragonflies.

Some realtor bought the ground
to create suburban concrete
and tidy lawns with Bradford pears.
I wonder if he knows
the Little Dipper is not for sale
and the stars need to stay put.

Pat Durmon

Ireland Castle with Bull by Jane E. Allen

TURNED-OVER SKY

Now looking at this evening sky, I swear
fine sand has settled on each wisp of cloud,
for gold lights up low-lying moisture shroud
as sun sends rays of shooting light to where
the waiting ground blends orange and oyster shades
in deepest place that night can hunker
down.
How soon? How soon will blue sky lose its crown
and more rain fall upon wet dells and glades?
       Light tugs at its last tether rope in vain,
       enticing wild black stallions of the sky
       to stampede out across my world as rain.
       I, shunning soaking, soon attempt to fly
       into my refuge of the safe and sane,
       yet know dark clouds turn over by and by.

Bonnie Stucki Gudmundson

COUNTRY CABIN

His daddy's daddy built a home
Hand hewn from Southern wood
Tools now rusted hang unused
A bygone era gone for good
His faithful dog sleeps under crumbling steps
Protecting what little legacy is left.

Laurie Boulton

48

FALLEN OAK

When our oak fell
it was all the moments of a hundred years
crashing
leaving space
that leaf and line and color tried to fill
but still
the space remained
a tall and shining emptiness
shaped like a tree
and yet it seems to me
the oak space
spreading branch and cloud of leaf
stands firmer than the oak
and safe from falling now
forever.

Malu Graham

DELAWARE

Snow geese are blanketing
January cornfields
Warming winter with down

Nancy Watts

Snow fritters away
Rendered nil in moonlight grill –
Ice staccatos flash.

Thomas McDaniel

Freshly fallen leaves
litter brown field; cool lilting
breezes spin a reel.

Thomas McDaniel

THE LAST DAY
(through Carolyn's eyes)

There's plenty of time.
I should have chosen the nail polish earlier,
        I suppose,
but I kept forgetting to put the fabric sample
        in my purse.
This morning, as luck would have it, I remembered
and took the swatch with me to the manicurist.
The match was difficult, but I think the shade is
        perfect.
I know the whole clan will be dressed to the nines
for the wedding. And I want John to be proud of me.
Well, the whole thing took forever, but finally
the color match appeared just right and my nails dried.

Lacquer looks different in a bottle than it does
on your nails, take my word. And different wet than dry.
I dashed back to the apartment to finish packing—
something else I should have done earlier – I know,
        I know—
then took the towncar to the airport where I saw
Laura had already arrived, mercifully. We talked.
Poor John is working on his flight plan.
I notice he has the cane with him and is limping.
I can tell he's relieved to see me; we are running late.
I'm surprised to see darkness coming on already.
Still, it's comforting to know the flight's just a short hop –
only thirty miles or so, I believe.
John's new plane is slick, but there's not a lot of room
where my sister and I will ride, in the back with the bags.
John says the visibility report is favorable
so Laura and I can load up. He'll start the engine
and we'll be on our way to Martha's Vineyard.

I hope my dress isn't wrinkling too badly…
Oh, well… (sigh). There's still plenty of time

Florence Bruce

From: *Tennessee Voices*

EARLY OZARK MORNING

morning sun and lake
touch gently becoming one
rippling molten gold

Diane Stefan

MOTHER OF OKLAHOMA

Ellie's young son, Ben, yelled, "Papa," when tall lanky Jim,
hat in hand, walked into the depot at Comanche, OK. Ellie
and Ben were dusty and smelling of tobacco smoke from
the long train ride from Fort Worth. The next hours took
them down wagon-track roads in an open wagon seated
on a spring-board seat. The bed of the wagon held lumber
and perched on top was Ellie's camel-back trunk with her
prized possessions. Ben sank down between Jim and Ellie
but soon laid his head down in his mama's lap and went
to sleep. Never in her wildest imagination had city-bred
Ellie thought of the hardships as she dreamed of her New
Life in the New Frontier. They were headed for the camp
of about twenty tents, where families waited for the
President to sign the papers for the Land Opening.
The tents looked inviting after the ride across the prairie
and Ellie found offered protection from the blazing sun
and wind-swept blizzards, both common in Southwest
Oklahoma. Ellie and other young wives washed clothes at
the bend of the creek, which provided plenty of crystal
clear water. The iron kettle set upon rocks with a hot fire
provided boiling water. With lye-soap, rub-boards, and ropes
stretched for a make shift clothes-lines, the laundry was
done and the young women visited, sang songs, let the kids
run and play, and made the most of each day, as they made-do
with what they had. And they talked. They talked up a school,
a church, a Post Office, and a General Store. Ellie told the
stories of early-day Oklahoma, over and over again. I wish
she was still here to tell them again. The pioneer women
like Ellie, not only gave birth to a brood of children, another
way of life, the group as a whole was the
Mother of Oklahoma.

Vera Long

FLEETING

Snatches of dreams
slip through my consciousness.
I try to catch them,
but they vanish
like precious jewels snatched
by thieves in the night.

Susanne Leeds

WONDERMENT OF DAWN

Through soft night shadows
and muted echoes,
the imminence of dawn
can be felt: unseen stirrings...
incautious movement
of a bird...wings whirring.
A little stream hushed
by the prevailing mood
as it creeps from pool to pool.
God's creatures hold their breath
in the stillness of its depths.

No time to add hours to my
dreams for dawn is coming:
the restless woodland is taking shape...
every creek-washed stone, every twig,
every trembling leaf, every blossom,
as a stain of saffron in the east
begins to steep the earth.
In the languid glow

of morning silence,
I blow out the kerosene lantern
as dawn chases away veils of darkness.

From a farm
along the dusty lane
rises the loud derisive
challenge of a rooster...
as if in mockery
of the extinguished flame.

Anne-Marie Legan

White Peacock, Okeechobee, Florida, by AnneMarie Dyer

FOOL'S GOLD

Go west, young man. Go west,
John Lane Soule proclaimed.
Find rivers of sparkling gold,
mountains of silver veins,
an open door to wealth,
the key in every hand.

Fame and fortune foretold,
west they flocked toward his call,
with their last dollar, last dream,
to stake claim on a plot,
breathe the air of winners,
bury their loser's past.

Dreams, elusive to grasp,
rainbows, pots of gold fade.
Reality, rasping,
bares man, strips the dream,
leaving truth, bones bleached,
like rock strewn on the sand.

Sarah Hull Gurley

RANDOM POEM

Random thoughts
have a way
of coming out
like small poems

Brett Taylor

WHEN HER MUSIC PLAYED
Dedicated to the memory of Helen Forrester

Across the keyboard Helen's fingers flew,
each measure ending in a stately roll.
The congregation's favorites she knew,
she struck the willing keys with heart and soul.

> For fifty years
>   her music
>   brought God
>   down to earth.

At each revival she performed the hymns
that brought folks down the aisles and to their knees.
She taught church music by her notes and deeds.
Across the keyboard Helen's fingers flew.

Frances Brinkley Cowden

Photo by AnneMarie Dyer

STUDENT FEATURE

Self Portrait by Jacob Call, Grade 10

OBSESSION

Obsession; such a simple word that means so much
And no one really understands to the full extent
Until they see it with their own eyes
Or until they see it in themselves
Until nothing matters in the world
Accept one person or thing alone
Until compulsive preoccupation
Takes over your life
And clouds your mind
And you can't remember your life before
And you can't imagine what life would be
Without your obsession. It's like a legal drug
The longer you obsess
The more addicted you become.

Courtney Watts, Grade 8

NIGHT

tired
in the dark
almost asleep thinking
slowly drifting away with the night

Whitney Lauren Brinkley, Grade 11

THE ONE

In the darkest hour
Of the Twilight Zone
There is a boy
That stands alone.
He does not weep
He does not cry
He just stands there
And he sighs.
He is bullied
Here and there
But he just waits
And he stares.
He waits for the one
The one that's right
The one with glee
The one with a smile
The one that's fun
The one that will
Help him up.

Christopher Watts Grade 6

HAIKU

Summer is too hot.
I am not sweating today.
I jumped in the pool.

Cameron Hidayat, Grade 3

59

WIND

Over hill and slope
Under rock and stone,
Lives something unknown.
It whispers:

Around the earth I perceive all
Around the world I travel through
Around and around I wave my
Pattern unending intertwining

I fear nothing, not pain nor death.
I feel all things, the trees the moss.
I taste everything, the warm spring flower
The late autumn leaves.

Running away always to return,
Running through meadow and plain,
Running and leaping at all times never
Killed nor broken.

I am unyielding.
I am everlasting.
I am impervious.
I am wind.

Navid Nia, Grade 7

SPIDERS

Small and hairy,
Poisonous fangs,
I don't like them.
Deadly bites of doom!!
Eats insects
Really fascinating
Super smart!

Pijom Nia, Grade 5

RAISINS

My dad likes raisins
Hundreds of plump
Juicy Sun Maid® raisins.
Those are the kinds he likes.
Yep! He likes raisins.

Mila Lauren Brinkley, Grade 2

Art by Sandra Corona
61

Bad Hair Day by AnneMarie Dyer

A BAD DAY

I am having a bad day.
My pencil broke.
My book mark is torn.
My lipstick has glue in it.
My crayon is broken.
I am very mad.
I am having a bad day.

Cecilia Snow, Grade 3

EAT YOUR HEART OUT, FRED ASTAIRE

Jo Anne Allen

"How old are you?" the young man questioned.

Lorella's hazel eyes twinkled. "Sixty-four."

There was a brief pause. "Are you sure this is the right class? I mean…look around. The average age is twenty. Lady, I teach punk dancing. I really don't think you're in any kind of shape to break-dance, to do the jumps, to endure the…,"

"Young man," Lorella interrupted. "I paid my fee to be here. I want to learn this crazy new stuff that my grandson loves to watch. I want to perform in a recital when this class is over. My grandson will be twenty-two in six weeks. The class is six weeks. This is his birthday present from me. It's important."

The young instructor could not help but grin from ear to ear. "A recital? I'm not teaching piano, Lady. We refer to it in the 21st century as a *performance*. And yes…that is the goal of the class. We perform on stage in front of whomever you want to invite."

"Then I'm in the right class," Lorella said, exposing her perfect set of false teeth.

The young man brushed through his wild blonde hair with both hands and then tilted his head back in an effort to find the correct words that would not offend his newest student. He looked into her large hazel eyes that were magnified by her bifocals.

"Did you sign a release form that doesn't hold the school liable for any damages?"

"For any serious injuries?" he finally asked.

"Yes. Young man…is it that odd that a woman of my *maturity* wants to learn the dance steps to modern music?" Lorella asked seriously.

The instructor burst out laughing. "I'm leery about older students trying stuff they haven't done in decades. Things break a lot easier on you than anyone else in here. But hey! You inspire me. I say go for it."

"You'd be surprised what good shape I'm in. I have a trampoline at home and do flips on it all the time. I might just prove to be the best dancer in this class," Lorella bragged.

"You can do a flip?" the instructor questioned.

"Certainly. I taught my grandson how to do 'em, too! It's easy if you do it everyday," Lorella said with conviction.

"You do a flip everyday?" he repeated in question form to verify her last statement.

"Yes. I do several. Both kinds. Front and back. Plus cartwheels. I learned long ago if you did it everyday, you'd never lose your nerve," she answered.

The young man nodded his head, somewhat impressed. She appeared honest. Who was he not to believe she was capable of what this class would demand?

"Okay, then," he said and then raised his arms to get the attention of the other twenty-six students in the large gym room.

"My name is Travis. I am the instructor for this class. It's an advanced dancing class teaching radical moves and daring stunts to add to the flavor of regular dancing. We do have a performance planned. It's the graduation party for completing the requirements. You will also receive a certificate acknowledging that you are now ...drum roll, please....*An authentic, outrageous, modern dance individual.*"

And so the class began. Lorella was over-whelmed by the physical requirements but she was a

64

trooper. At 5'4", she weighed 140 pounds. Her face was laced with wrinkles and looking at her, one could see that she was a beauty in her day. Her white head of hair replaced the once brunette locks. She did appear to be in great shape for her age and amazed everyone, especially Travis, that she was game for anything dished out. She tried it all and worked at it until she could do it. One would only speculate at the hours she put in after class was over. This was the hardest thing she's ever done in her life and sixty-four years is a lot of life. She was on a mission.

She had tunnel vision when it came to this class. Her entire goal was to be *good* at it. She didn't want to be known as an old lady who reverted back to her teenage years. She wanted to be good...real good. This would be the best birthday present she could ever give to her grandson. He was going to be so surprised. That vision alone kept her going.

The class was beyond grueling, at five nights a week for two hours at a time. Stretching was the important part and that came as no surprise. She was glad she kept up with her exercises through the years. This class demanded splits and limberness beyond her capabilities. She even surprised herself with her agility.

During this time she lost ten pounds, strained every muscle in her aging body and maintained her optimistic attitude to the brim. She would often soak in the bathtub for hours and count her bruises. She was tempted to skip a class or two but she never did. You could set your watch by her and soon won the heart of every student in the class. Her nickname was '*unstoppable Lorella.*'

They learned to respect her desire to learn. Although amazed that her generation would even listen to hard rock, they often laughed when she chimed in to tunes played over and over. Her sense of humor was the icing on the cake. Her imitation of Michael Jackson doing the moonwalk brought the entire class to their knees. She was contagious and her determination unbelievable. She attracted people like a magnet.

"Lorella? Why is this class so important for you?" one of the young females wanted to know early on.

"It's my birthday present to my grandson. He loves watching it. It sure looks fun. Of course, sky diving looks fun until you jump out of a perfectly good airplane and wonder what the heck you were thinking," Lorella said and grinned.

"Your grandson?"

"He's the greatest grandson in the world," Lorella said without hesitating as her facial expression turned quite serious. "He's the love of my life. I practically raised him. He'll be twenty-two soon, and somehow I think him witnessing his sixty-four year old grandma dancing in the style he loves more than anything would be the best birthday present he ever got. It's gonna' be a big surprise!"

As Lorella dressed for the performance, she shook her head thinking about what she would be doing soon. She would jump in the air, fall on the floor and land on her back and then dance around using her neck muscles for pivoting. She would do the splits and take three lunges forward and do a handspring. This would all be over the course of an hour. She was glad she kept up with aerobic exercises from her childhood. Somehow, she knew her future would demand another cartwheel late in life.

Would it all be worth it? She thought about her favorite quote she lived by…"*Whatever we do on Earth echoes in all eternity*" Would this be an echo worth hearing over and over?

And so the performance began.

Lorella charmed the audience with her stamina and ability to keep up with the others. At her age, she certainly stood out. This was her shining hour. This was why she was put on Earth. She didn't care about making an impression on anyone but her grandson.

And so she did. He watched from the front row, with his mouth gaped open, at every incredible move Lorella made. The whole class was now aware of the importance of her mission.

Travis was ecstatic when the entire audience honored her with a standing ovation. He said a few words about how hard his students worked and what they have achieved. And then he did something out of character. He handed the microphone to Lorella.

"Don't you have something you'd like to say?" he asked as he encouraged her to come forward.

Unintimidated, Lorella took a deep breath and swallowed before she spoke.

Pointing to her grandson in the front row, she said, "This is my grandson whom I love dearly. Today he's twenty-two. Six months ago, he was in a car accident that left him in that wheelchair. Before that, he was a dancer. A very good dancer. It was his career. *It was his life.* He doesn't know I heard him say this, but three months into therapy, I was watching him. He was so discouraged. The therapist asked him what it would take to get him to try again…to give it a lot more than what he was giving it. Do you remember what you said, Son?"

You could have heard a pin drop. The microphone was taken to the confined young man and, with tears streaking down his face, he said, "Yes, Grandma. I'll learn to walk again when my grandma can dance like I used to."

YELLOW PAGES ROMANCE

Carl Dana

I met Big City Sid six months ago at a SOFA dance--that's the Singles Over Forty Association. I was doing the last steps of a Latin Hustle with Herb Arnold. Sid was beside us, dipping Angelina Buonofortuna way over backwards when, suddenly, Angelina's dancing spikes slipped. Her head bounced twice as she went down, and Sid belly-flopped on her.

Thanks to Angelina's bulk, Sid was unhurt. Herb pulled him up. Thanks to her airbag hairdo, a lacquered bouffant thing that matched her width, Angelina was also unhurt. I helped her up and caught Sid enjoying my decolletage, his nostrils flaring. He smiled guiltily, and looked away.

Angelina went to the ladies' room--to spray her hair, she said. Bertha Becker said Angelina wet herself when she fell. She must have, because I didn't see her any more that night.

Shortly after Angelina disappeared, Sid asked me to dance. Then again, and again. He was easy to follow. His hustles and lindys reminded me of Gene Kelly. His two-step, of Ray Bolger. His waltz, Fred Astaire. But he looked like Jimmy Cagney's George M. Cohan with his solid build, medium height, and impish smile. He had dark hair graying at the temples, hazel eyes and thick dark brows. Definitely Jimmy Cagney, with hazel eyes.

On our first date, during the week, he was certainly the gentle Jimmy Cagney of *Yankee Doodle Dandy*, and not the James Cagney of *White Heat*. We went to a three-star Japanese restaurant. He asked me questions about myself; he called me by my name: "Myrna, have you ever....?" and "Myrna, this...Myrna, that...." He told me his hobby was gourmet cooking. By the end of the evening, I was charmed and intrigued by this man who spouted phrases I seemed to recall from *Gourmet* and other food magazines I've seen in beauty parlors. So I accepted an invitation to dinner at his place.

"Any ethnic cuisine you want," he said.

Ethnic foods I know and love raced through my mind. "Any?"

"Try me," he challenged, "but Hungarian is my specialty."

"All right, Hungarian."

"You got it! Friday, 7 p.m." He handed me his card.

The next morning Isabelle called. "Myrna, oh, Myr-na."

"All right, Isabelle," I said. "Spare me the histrionics."

"You had dinner with Big City Sid last night?" she oozed delightedly.

"Yes. How did you find out?" I countered.

"Bella saw you," she said.

"Big Mouth Bella should write a gossip column," I said. "So I had dinner with a man. Since when is that front page news?"

"Oh, but Sid is not just ANY man, Myrna, and," she paused, "he invited you to one of his home-cooked gourmet dinners, right?"

"What?" I was angry now and made a mental note to tell Bella off. "Does Bella still carry around her mail-order eavesdropping device wherever she goes? Anyway, so what if he did?"

"No, Myrna, Bella didn't tell me. I happen to know that's how Sid operates." Isabelle was on stage again. "Oh, Myrna, Myr-na…"

"Enough, Isabelle. Give me the bad news already," I said. "Sid's married?"

"Oh, Myrna, worse than that."

I blurted my first thought, "He's gay?"

"No, no," Isabelle laughed. "He's widowed, has three grown children, two grandchildren; he's the northeast sales manager for Teepee Toys;...."

"He's a pedarest!"

"Nooo!"

"So?" I wondered what could be wrong with this man. "He drives a nice car, dresses well, plays tennis, is a good dancer, is personable,...."

"Oh, Myrna, he's a horny vampire! He uses food and drink to seduce women. He's a Don Juan in-cu-BUS! But he can't cook. He orders meals from the Yellow Pages. He's a stud, S-T-U-D! X-RAY-TED, and he likes plump ones, Myrna, so beware! Be-A-WARE, Myr-na!"

I snapped at her, "Thanks for the advice." Then lied, "But you haven't seen me since I lost 15 pounds, so I won't be one of his trophies."

I hung up the phone and mused aloud, "Then again...but I won't tell you, Isabelle."

His apartment was clean, decorated in soft pastels, more feminine than masculine--part of his technique, I surmised. He had set a lovely table with candles and flowers, and Ravel's *Bolero* was playing softly on his stereo.

Dinner began with a light *paprikash* salad of cucumber and sour cream on a bed of arugula and red Romaine lettuce. Then we had a goose liver risotto, with peas, mushrooms, cheese, butter and other flavors. Then *Paloc*, a mutton soup. It was delicious and I asked what was in it besides potato, lemon and sour cream.

"I'll tell you later, Myrna. But now, the next course--*Szekely* goulash, a favorite of mine," he said as he put a paprika-laden dish before me.

It was superb. Again, he was too busy to tell me the ingredients other than the obvious ones: pork spare ribs, sauerkraut, caraway seeds, sour cream and lots of paprika.

Finally, we had *cafe au lait*, to wash down *Pozsony* Squares, a sour cream and poppy seed pastry.

We danced another ten minutes or so. Then, fearful that I was beginning to mellow and might indeed become his second dessert, I said my goodbyes.

70

"But subways are dangerous--" he said, "for pretty ladies at this hour. Stay. In the morning I'll serve you breakfast in bed--fresh bagels, lox, blintzes--one of the city's best delis is on this block."

"No thank you, but I want to repay you, Sid. How about a Northern Italian dinner next Friday? My place."

My dinner was superb, thanks to Giullietta's Cucina. Only I did some research and knew what went into each dish. Sid was impressed and invited me to a Czechoslovakian meal at his place the next Friday. A week later, we had Ceylonese at my place.

For the next several months we also dined out, beginning with the "A"'s in the Yellow Pages; we went dancing, saw some good films, visited museums, and walked. We dated rather casually, he thought; rather seriously, I knew.

Now Sid knows I know he can't cook. But he doesn't know that I fooled him into thinking I can, which I probably can, but I won't. Why bother with the mess when there are thousands of ethnic restaurants in this city? We're still working our way through them. I can't wait till we get to the "GR"'s; I love Greek food almost as much as Lucy Giullietta's Italian food.

Especially during the holidays, Lucy Giullietta makes sweet ricotta fritters she calls "sfinge," her quick version of *zeppole*. She gave me the recipe. Frankly, I think any woman who makes her own desserts is just too lazy to drive to the bakery. But, if you're lazy, try making them--for real! And let me know.

Oh, by the way, Sid and I got married when we finished the F's. We're honeymooning our way through the G's--sooo many wonderful restaurants in Berlin. Next week we'll be in Athens. I can't wait!

Eat your heart out, Is-a-BELLE!

LUCY GIULLIETTA'S SFINGE

1/4 lb. (1 stick) butter, softened
1 egg
1/2 c. milk
1/2 c. ricotta cheese
1/4 c. sugar
1 1/2 c. flour
1 T. baking powder
1/2 t. salt
1 c. or more, powdered sugar
1 t. cinnamon
oil for frying

Beat till smooth the softened butter, egg, milk, sugar, ricotta, flour, baking powder and salt. In a large saucepan (fry pans splatter more) heat oil and fry tablespoons of batter till bubbly; turn with a slotted spoon and cook till golden. Drain on paper towels. Dust with powdered sugar and cinnamon. Serve hot.

Art by Sandra Corona

GEORGE

John E. Clemons

George was an unusual name for a horse, but then George was as good a name as Joe or Jim or any other. George was an exceptional horse, exceptional in that he was not handsome as far as horse looks go. His head was too large, his ears too small and his eyes too deep. His body seemed out of proportion also; his withers were small, his rump was large and his tail was short.

Maybe, it was because of his large head that George was more intelligent than the other horses on the farm. John, who owned George, loved him and used him for his driving horse because he was so intelligent. John knew that wherever he went with George, George would get him safely home, even when John fell asleep after the many dances he and his date, Lasette, had danced at the town hall. They were celebrating the wedding of their mutual friends. John often fell asleep on the way home and he would wake up after he felt the buggy stop. There George would be at the barn door waiting patiently for John to wake up and unhitch him from the buggy. No matter where John went, George always knew the way home.

The mode of travel was changing in the early 1900's with the production of the automobile. The automobile had not arrived yet in John's small town.

The horse and buggy still remained the mode of travel in most rural areas. This made travel slower but quiet and romantic. Soon the Model T Ford would take over the roads.

It was in the spring of 1917 when Lasette and John went to visit friends five miles away. They had debated about going this far because the weather had been miserable. It would not stop raining.

John said, "Lasette, the rain doesn't bother George. I think he likes it. His big head and deep set eyes protect him from the rain and his small ears keep the water out. Do you mind going?"

"Okay, if George doesn't mind, John, and if it is okay with you then the rain won't bother me."

The rain continued all the way to their friend's house, making the five miles seem even longer. The evening was enjoyable and the lunch of chocolate cake and coffee still left a pleasant taste in John's mouth.

As they started home, the rainfall picked up in intensity and force. John had put on the side and front curtains to keep the rain off Lasette. This, however, limited their visibility.

John was confident George knew the way home, so he and Lasette, in their makeshift house, began concentrating on each other. Lasette's kisses were warm and inviting. They were paying little attention to the road, but George was paying attention.

Lasette said, "John, are we home already? George has stopped. He is just standing in the road."

John looked out but could not see why George had stopped.

"George, giddy-up," John yelled, slapping the reins across George's large rump.

George wouldn't budge. Suddenly George started. He turned the buggy around, and headed in a different direction. Neither Lasette nor John could see where George was taking them. He seemed to be in a hurry and John did not try to stop him. They seemed to be riding for a very long time when the horse stopped again, however, this time it was at Lasette's home. There was a light burning in the kitchen, so John went in with Lasette. Her distraught parents were waiting in the kitchen.

"We were so worried about you. Your friends called and said the road by Overflow Creek was washed out. The water is high all along the creek."

"That's why George stopped" John said, "He knew that river was too high. George stopped and turned around on our way home. We didn't know why at the time. He sensed danger and took us to the high road," he told Lasette's parents.

"John, I think George deserves a good meal in our dry barn. It is too dangerous for you to be out. You stay here tonight," Fred said.

The next morning Fred and John went to look at the washout. There was a large gully where the road had been. John and Lasette would have drowned had George not known there was danger.

George lived a long life. The extra care John heaped on him may have helped. There are other stories of George's exceptional intelligence. On one occasion John's cows got into the neighbor's pasture. George went into the neighbor's pasture and retrieved only John's cows and none of the neighbors. He did this in a dense fog.

John was always amazed at his horse with the large head, small ears, deep set eyes, small withers and the large rump. It seemed his intelligence went through the entire horse, right to his short tail.

John always remembered the time George used his intelligent intuition to save his life and Lasette's on the night of the great downpour.

MY SPECIAL CHURCH DAY

N. E. Chapman

Not even the stiff white collar and the choking bow tie kept me from being the happiest ten-year old kid in the whole world that Sunday morning. After smoothing the top of my unruly red hair with a bit of spit, I was ready for my Confirmation.

I really didn't understand what Confirmation meant except Mama said I'd be eligible to be named a full-member of the church. What pleased me most was that my skinny knees would be hidden with long trousers. *Long trousers!* For the first time, I could throw those short pants away, or maybe give them to a younger kid. It won't be long before I can get my driver's license, I thought, and wondered if Mama would let me drive her shiny, new Ford

Mama told me to sit in a chair and not to move while she climbed the stairs to get ready for church. After squirming in the chair a few minutes, I remembered I hadn't fed the chickens. I ambled to the chicken yard and the hot morning sun stirred up the awful smell the chickens made. After feeding them, I wandered off to the pine grove a few hundred feet from the house.

I heard a little moan that sounded like a kitten. Then I saw him. He looked me in the eyes as if I'd set the trap to catch his small hind leg. His shiny black coat had a white stripe down his back and he was trying to raise his tail. I suspected what he wanted to do.

"Don't you dare!" I warned. "Take it easy. I'm gonna' get you out of there."

As I reached for the trap, he bared his little teeth and raised his tail again. "Now don't do it, nor bite, my little friend. I'm gonna' save you." I tried to stay in front of him while I released him from the trap. He lay there weak and crying like a baby.

I hurried home for a box and found my mother had already left for church. I guess she thought I got tired of waiting and had gone without me. With the box under my arm, I hurried back and put my little friend in it. I ran back to the house and slid the box under my bed.

"Now you stay there until I get back Then I'll find something for you to eat."

I hurried along the few blocks to the church. The place was packed with mostly gray-haired people. I saw Mama squeezed in tight between Mrs. Goodwill and Mrs. Fellowgood. "Hi, Mama," I said. "I'm here and ready for my Confirmation."

All the people in that row began moving to another part of the church. I wondered what was wrong. Could it be I carried the smell of the chicken yard? First Mama looked right, then she looked left, and then she looked all around her. I thought she hadn't seen me "Mama, I'm here," I said again.

Then Mama looked straight at me. I'll never forget the weird expression on her face. "Who are you?" she asked

I couldn't believe my own mother didn't recognize me. *But she was my mother.*

"Tommy," I said. "I'm Tommy, your own boy child, your own kid. Don't you know me? I'm here for my Confirmation."

Mama held her handkerchief to her nose and made a terrible face. "I don't know who you are," she said. "Go home. Your mother may be wondering where you are."

Then she fled from the church like a group of devils were after her. I looked around the church and saw everyone rushing to get outside in the summer air.

I didn't know why they were in such a hurry to leave.

When I reached home, Mama sat in the porch swing fanning herself. "There's a terrible odor in the house. It smells just like the boy I thought was you, at the church.

Was that you?"

Saying nothing, I trudged to my room. I sank to my bare knees, wondering if I'd ever get those long trousers. My friend was still in the box under my bed. My friend smiled at me as if he wore a tantalizing perfume.

My little friend remembered me.

A POEM I FIRST THOUGHT OF IN MEMPHIS

the morning light
creeps through the window shades
but the rooster no longer crows
as it did when I was seven or eight
and the city seemed as far to me
as the bottom of the ocean viewed by a raven

Brett Taylor

Art by Lenna Frye

FOUR FRIENDS, AN IMPROVISATION

Marguerite Thoburn Watkins

Once in the Terai of Nepal, the space where cultivated fields and the lush vegetation of the valley meet the evergreen forests of the mountains, grew a fruit tree. To the beauty of the tree's twisted silvery bark and symmetrical sap-green leaves, was added, in the spring, a profusion of scented blossoms. The flowers were replaced in season by fruit with such rich sweet juice and tender flesh that every creature desired it. This fruit was neither mango nor peach, although it had the smooth skin and brilliant red-orange coloring of the first and the sweet fragrance of the second. The tree was unique; the hill people said that it had been planted by the valley gods, bequeathed to their representative, the *raja* of this small kingdom in which it grew.

Now the *raja* had a beautiful wife, the beloved of his heart, and a daughter more lovely than any flower. It was his joy to give pleasure to his queen and the young princess so he saved the succulent fruit for them, and for that reason a guard stood beside the tree by day and slept against its trunk by night. The king told him that no one else could eat fruit from this one tree for the supply was limited.

The *raja* had a fine white elephant who carried his master in a *howdah* for ceremonial parades. For these occasions an artist painted patterns on the forehead of the rare and faithful beast and his *mahout* decked him with silk hangings. The elephant smelled the ripe fruit. Delicately he stepped over the pasture on his huge feet, and kneeling before the guard, bowed his head as he respectfully asked that he be permitted to pick just one apple. It was not an apple, but that is what he called it. He said it would be no trouble be-cause his trunk could easily reach the lower branches. Regretfully the guard told him of the king's command, for a white elephant is the most loyal and deserving of all creatures.

The next day the chieftain of the langur monkey band came; the summer breezes carried the scent of the miraculous fruit far into the jungles. He started to climb the trunk and his hairy hand had just reached a fruit when the guard seized a *lathi* and threatened him, commanding him to jump down from the *raja's* tree. The wily monkey spoke of Hanuman the monkey god and of his own sacred status among animals. But the guard stood firm; he knew his duty.

In the evening as dusk fell, a shy hare crept out from his burrow to nibble the clover in the field. He hoped also to come upon a fallen piece of the succulent fruit. In a humble voice he told the watchman of his longing for a taste – so tantalizing was its fragrance. The guard's heart was touched by the hare's modesty and he would gladly have knocked down a piece for him and his kids, but he kindly told him also that the fruit from this one tree was reserved for the royal family.

Later that week an odd visitor crawled by. It was an old tortoise; he had lived in the Terai for years, surely a patriarch with many descendents. The guard watched the creature take the whole day to cross the field, pulling his head under his shell in alarm every time even a bird flew by. Finally he reached the feet of the king's servant. The old fellow bravely stretched out his head and in a cracked, creaking voice asked the guard for a piece of fruit. The young man was abashed, for he knew that respect must be given to old age and to the helpless. The watchman decided to refuse the tortoise without seeming to refuse him; he gave him permission to have what he could pick for himself. For, he reasoned, a tortoise can neither reach up nor climb.

The guard did not notice the hare and the monkey resting under the evergreens at the edge of the field. And wallowing in the nearby stream was the white elephant.

Then up rose the elephant, carefully washing the mud off his alabaster hide. He offered to lift the old tortoise; but when his trunk curled firmly about the large shell the tortoise could not quite reach the bough.

Then the langur monkey came out of the bushes and climbed on the elephant's back to hold up the tortoise. But even elephant, monkey and tortoise could not quite pick the tempting clusters on the lower branches.

Quietly the hare crept from his hiding place and stood by the white elephant. He whispered to him to lean down to hear his plan. "The monkey must climb onto your head, and then you must lift me with your trunk to stand on his head and the tortoise to stand on mine. My long ears will prop him up straight."

The balance was precarious but the tower held steady – elephant, monkey, hare and tortoise. The tor-toise snipped off one, two, three, four pieces of luscious fruit. They were his because he picked them himself, but he took enough to share with his three friends.

Unknown to anyone, the *raja* and his wife and daughter were walking in the forest. The watchman fell to the ground in terror because his Lord had seen that he had neglected his duty. But the child clapped her hands with pleasure at the strange sight. The king and queen smiled, for the elephant and his friends had shown their daughter that it is through cooperation with one another that we achieve our goals. So unlike each other in nature and talents, the four beasts had accomplished together what no one of them could achieve alone. The king lifted up the quaking guard and gave him a new order: each year when the gardeners picked fruit for the royal family, the elephant, monkey, hare and tortoise must have a portion also. Surely he and his subjects had much to learn from these four friends.

Then he bade his noble white elephant kneel down so that he could speak into his ear. "I have always believed that you bring my kingdom good luck," he said, "because you were born as white as the ivory of your tusks. Now I know the true reason. You bring good fortune because you believe, as the seers tell us, that the greatest must hold up the least."

**View of the Serengeti (dots in the background are
animals) by Barbara B. Abbott**

A NEAT AND TIDY CRIME

Phylis Warady

Nancy paused just inside the door of Harvey Mosher's flat. She picked a path through discarded bits of red cellophane ringing the Boston rocker. Her eyes snagged upon the rocker's seat cushion which bore permanent indentations made by the elderly Vet's brittle bones.

Tears crowded her eyes. Mosher had been gassed in a long past war and had suffered severe bouts of asthma as a result. He'd sworn the lozenges that came wrapped in red cellophane had helped him breathe.

Last Monday though, they'd failed him. An ambulance had spirited him off to Veteran's Hospital where he'd died during the night.

Wednesday morning Nancy was dressing Josh, her wiggly toddler, when a petite woman tapped on her screen door.

"Greta Hiller?" Nancy asked.

The woman nodded curtly. She wore a tailored suit. Its violet hue matched her eyes. Nancy was glad she'd changed from her ratty terrycloth robe into a sundress.

"Come in," she invited, flinging open the door. "I half expected a call last night."

"I did get in last night," the woman admitted, "But I was too exhausted to phone. You received my wire?"

"Yes. Coffee? I was about to have a cup."

"No, thanks. I'm anxious to get into my Uncle's flat."

Balancing Josh on her hip, Nancy slid the key off its nail and handed it to her.

Greta Hiller did not reappear until midday. Nancy was bathing Josh.

"Will you be free soon? I've been going through my Uncle's personal effects and have questions."

"The screen door's unlatched. Come on in. As soon as I put Josh down for a nap, I'll fix lunch."

"Oh, I couldn't impose."

"There's no place to eat nearby."

"Very well then."

Greta's eyes inventoried the cramped kitchen in a manner that made Nancy feel as if she lived in a hovel. Stuffing beefsteak tomatoes with white tuna, she found herself wishing they didn't have to eat off the kitchen table.

Her guest sat rigidly erect on a straight-backed chair. "Tell me, Nancy, where did my Uncle keep his money?"

"His money?" The question stunned her. "I really don't know. He did have a coin purse. He kept it in his sweater pocket."

"A coin purse? I don't mean his loose change. I mean his money." She said money as if each letter were capitalized.

"He lived on a pension. There would not be much left over after he paid rent and bought groceries."

The violet eyes darkened as though a storm threatened. "I'm not stupid, Nancy. You had a key. I don't want trouble. If you tell me where he hid his money. I'll even give you a reward."

"How dare you?" Nancy's temper smoldered. "His doctor insisted I have a key. Someone had to check to make sure your uncle wasn't having an asthma attack. Someone had to call an ambulance when he got sick. Someone had to send you a telegram."

Totally unruffled, Greta Hiller said, "I don't mean to upset you. But if you didn't go through Uncle's papers, how did you know how to contact me?"

Mosher's niece didn't believe her. Nancy felt sick to her stomach.

"Mrs. Hiller, I cleaned out his fridge and washed his bedding. His sheets are in the dryer if you want them. I did not snoop. I got your address off a Christmas postcard lying on the table beside his rocker."

The nerve of the woman!

"Nancy, I'm not accusing you of anything. Uncle distrusted banks, so if he had any money, it had to be in his apartment. Perhaps you're right though. I went through all his junk with a fine-toothed comb."

She set her fork on her empty plate. "I had counted on finding his stash. Ah well, here's the key. I'm booked on the night flight."

Nancy stared at the key resting on the plastic tablecloth. "What about funeral arrangements?"

"Money doesn't grow on trees. It'd be different if he'd left me something. As it is, I'm out my travel expenses."

"But you're all the family he had."

Greta Hiller shrugged. "He was a Veteran. Let the government bury him."

"And his personal things?"

"That trash? Take what you want; burn the rest."

After Greta Hiller left, Nancy decided to fold Mr. Mosher's bedding before Josh woke from his nap.

She pulled the Vet's pillow from the dryer. And sneezed. Darn it! One of its seams must have popped. Too bad she hadn't noticed before she'd tossed it in. Now she'd have a mess of feathers to clean. And his sheets were too thin to be of use, even as rags. Nancy tossed the bedding in the incinerator and lit a match.

When Josh woke, they went for their daily walk. Coming home through the alley, she was still keyed up. It taxed her patience whenever her curious toddler paused to examine something. As they reached the incinerator, Josh broke free from her grasp and scooped up a scrap of paper off the ground.

"Don't you dare put that in your mouth!"

Catching hold of him, Nancy straightened his fingers one by one. Ignoring his wail of protest, she opened the iron incinerator door, intending to toss in the scrap. But a curious crackle stayed her hand. Faint recognition set cogs spinning. She smoothed the disreputable-looking scrap. A crisp twenty-dollar bill!

Dazed, she put Josh in his fenced-in yard. Thoughts rising and falling like a roller coaster track, she began to laugh. Her laughter held a touch of hysteria. Mr. Mosher had stashed some money. Inside his pillow of all places! And she'd inadvertently burnt it up.

"Take what you want, burn the rest," Greta Hiller had said.

Nancy stared at the twenty-dollar bill. Then, as slowly, as magically, as dawn breaking on a new day, her face lightened. Just enough to buy flowers for the old Vet's grave.

IDENTITY CRISIS

Whether the structure is splendid or crass,
Wrought of wood, brick, stucco or glass,
Most modern architecture,
Invites this conjecture.
Should one pray, deposit or buy gas?

Phylis Ann Warady

Gleaners, **Elizabeth Howard, 884289-47-9**
Grandmother Earth, 2005.

Review by Daniel Dahlquist

In poem after poem, Elizabeth Howard shakes me. Her subject matter--rape, murdered babies, suicide--is disturbing, but it is her fine eye, her attention to detail, that convinces. She possesses an acute sensitivity, one that penetrates to a meaning deep inside, and this is poetry. In "Blue Flowers" Howard has taken the persona of a husband who grieves for his son. We feel the full weight of D.H. Lawrence's recognition that there is something deeper than love in a human being, namely one's sense of justice. This speaker accuses an abusive mother with a startling, righteous anger, in straight-forward language and powerful images. We have a whole tragic novel in a single poem.

Elizabeth Howard is deceptively simple, and uses understatement well. "Lesson" achieves considerable power by capturing a believable human voice, a fearless country voice. The speaker shocks by looking squarely at an advancing predatory evil and refusing to look away.

Howard has the ability to evoke a world: In "Emancipation" we have a fine example of her skill in shaping personas and creating vivid characters in very few words. *Gleaners* sticks to the ribs. I have been given images I can't forget, and several of these may be found in Howard's poems on the Civil War. I think some of her characters are as powerful as those of the immortal Edgar Lee Masters in *Spoon Rivers Anthology*. *Gleaners* is regional poetry in the best sense: it casts a wide net.

JUDGES COMMENTS

Martha McNatt: Judging the Prose

I tried my best to judge the prose based upon interesting story line, writing style, sentence structure, and the quality of beginning and ending. It was fun but not easy.

~~~

Madelyn Eastlund: Judging the Poetry

It was a pleasure to read all the entries. As I think I mentioned I give several readings .. .spacing them to be sure I don't overlook one. I wind up with three piles. Those that were eliminated during the first reading (but I always read the batch again!). Those that are eliminated in the many other readings as I whittle down to the ten best. And then I lay aside for a day and when I read I sit in my comfy chair with a pot of tea beside me . . . and each is read aloud . . .

What do I look for when I am judging? The same things I look for when I receive submissions for my own magazine, *Harp-Strings Poetry Journal*. I call it a "poem to remember". Hard to explain but I recognize such a poem when I read it and hear it! . . . a poem I won't read once and turn the page and forget. A poem to read over again . . . and actually to enjoy even more with each reading. A poem that takes the reader into it. A poem the reader (or listener) experiences. The author hasn't "told" a story but has given it as a gift to the reader to move into. And such a poem starts right off with the first two lines enticing the reader in with the use of the words chosen that create a mood as the poem goes towards its conclusion. Oh, yes....about that conclusion. So many poets write very good poems until they come to the last two lines . . . and they throw the poem away by summarizing or just a flat ending.

Comments on Individual Winners

Losing the Farm: The poet is in control of this narrative from the first line: The rhythm, the rhymes and the story that is told. Reading it aloud is a pleasure. It reads so smoothly. A fine poem to read on the page and a fine poem to give as a reading . . .sure to hold the audience.

Geese: From the first line the poem held my interest. At first I wondered who was doing the saying . . . but as the poem went on I just followed the monologue not thinking about 'who' was saying but drawn deeply into the imagery in each stanza . . . the little pictures that were piling up . . . and some of the phrases "embers remember words" and "orchards are only "moon-wishes" created a strange mood that kept me involved . . . 'trees are really owls .. . and then the end that made it all a unit . . . and the "geese" . . . I read it aloud and heard it's haunting -- sometimes a poem looks good on paper and carries thoughts or images into the mind but fails the "read aloud" test. For me an award wining poem must never fail that test!   This was beautifully written! It would also mesmerize an audience listening.

Cottonwoods: A beautifully crafted sonnet, there is imagery and I not only see but I hear cottonwoods whisper .... wind swishing in mournful tones.. river play a liquid song . . . ghostly drums ...bony chimes . . . read it aloud and you hear the magic rhythm ...the rhymes not intrusive .... a mood that brings the listener or the reader into the poem experiencing it.

When the Moon Was Unreachable This nostalgic poem didn't "tell" about that once upon a time called "yesterday" it gave yesterday in each line . . . running boards, gravel roads . . and a family that I could see. By the time the poem ended Mama and Daddy and the narrator were real to me. I don't know if the poet was man or woman but I know that the narrator of this poem is a woman who remembered "kidding and hugging" . . . and "giggling".

Shiloh I've never been to Shiloh but this poet took me along . . . not only on the walk the poet took but also to the Shiloh of the Civil War. This poem written on two levels that blended was so well crafted and ended with a "take away" .. .It didn't just end the walk . . . it didn't give a sermon . . . but it did have a take away . . . to think about . .. to see Shiloh perhaps in a different way . . .

Standing in the Dark. This is a poignant poem, and the narrator is so very real....both as narrator and as the child who had so many questions. Again, this is a poem that breathes on the page and lifts to move into the reader's head. I could have been the child -- I was actually for the space of time of reading the poem.

The Art of Peace and Origami . . . I loved those last two lines!

Thank you so much for giving me the privilege of judging -- and it is a privilege to judge...I think the judge of any competition also comes out a winner....

MEET THE JUDGES

Patricia L. W. Crocker, Ed.D, has retired from Memphis City Schools. Originally from Kingsport, Tennessee, she has been a resident of Memphis since 1978. Upon retirement, Pat embraced two hobbies: (1) writing fiction, non-fiction, and poetry and (2) enjoying the outdoors with her two energetic dogs. She is presently the treasurer of the Poetry Society of Tennessee and a member of Tennessee Writers Alliance. She also enjoys tutoring two students and visiting with her two children and four grandchildren.

Madelyn Eastlund, Beverly Hills, FL, a retired instructor of Fiction Writing and Poetry Writing for Central Florida Community College, and also for Withlacoochee Institute, is in the middle of her sixteenth year as editor of two Verdure Publications magazines: *Poets Forum Magazine; Harp-Strings Poetry Journal.* She is immediate past president of the NFSPS, past president of Florida State Poets Assoc., and is in her 21st year as the Poetry Workshop Director for the Gingerbread Poets. For over forty years her fiction, essays, and poetry have appeared in various magazines, journals, anthologies, and newspapers She is now in the middle of her 17th year publishing *Harp-Strings Poetry Journal* and *Poets' Forum Magazine* and in the 22nd year as The Gingerbread Poets Workshop Director.

Martha McNatt, Jackson, TN, is a former teacher, and director of the Child Nutrition Program for Madison County Schools. She is the author of *Feeding the Flock,* a cookbook for church kitchens, published by Bethany House, *A Heritage Revisited,* a commissioned work by First Christian Church, Jackson, TN, and *Grandmother's Face In The Mirror,* a collection of grandmother stories, published by Main Street Publishing of Jackson .This year, (2005) She has edited a cookbook *Friends Fare,* published by Friends of the Jackson Madison County Library. Her work has appeared in each of the Grandmother Earth anthologies, in *Grandmother Earth's Healthy and Wise Cookbook,* and in Life Press's *Our Golden Thread.* Martha is a member of the

Jackson Circle Branch of the National League of American Pen Women.

Tom McDaniel, professionally know as Thomas W. McDaniel, is an attorney in Memphis, TN. He has been President, and is Poet Laureate Emeritus, Life Member and Honorary member of PST. He has given programs on and published many haiku.

Lucile Roberts Ray, Memphis, TN, has won many writing awards Her new book *Gifts: Extraordinaries from an Ordinary Life* contains poetry and prose.

~~~

MEET THE STAFF

Mary Frances Broome lives in Germantown, TN,. She and Bill have two married children. She loves to serve as a volunteer in the office of Covenant United Methodist Church in Cordova, TN where they are active members. Mary Frances was employed with Shulton, Inc./American Cyanamid Company for 30 years, and was Plant Administrative Assistant at her retirement in 1993. She received the Certified Professional Secretary rating from the National Secretaries Association in 1979. After earning an Associate of Business Degree at Northwest Mississippi Junior College in 1982, she received a Bachelor of Business Degree in August 1985 at Memphis State University. Her favorite hobby is playing Bridge, especially Duplicate Bridge.

Frances Brinkley Cowden is founder of Grandmother Earth and Life Press. Grandmother Earth won the 1995 Business Environmental Award given by the city of Germantown, TN. Cowden received the Purple Iris Award in 2000 for outstanding contribution to the community through her publishing and the Life Press Writers' Conference. The Iris Awards are co-sponsored by the Memphis Branch of the National Organization of Business

Women. In 2001 she was selected as one of the 50 Women who Make a Difference by *Memphis Woman Magazine*. She is vice president of the Chickasaw Branch of NLAPW and a former president of PST.

Patricia Smith is editor of and critic for *Grandmother Earth* and other GEC and Life Press publications. She has won regional and national awards. She is treasurer of the NLAPW, Chickasaw Branch and an honorary member and a past president of PST.

E. Marcelle Zarshenas Nia, a Memphis attorney, has helped with the editing of Grandmother Earth publications since its beginning in 1993.

~~~~

CONTRIBUTORS

Common abbreviations used: PST, Poetry Society of Tennessee; NLAPW, National League of American Pen Women; NFSPS, National Federation of State Poetry Societies; PRA, Poets' Roundtable of Arkansas.

Barbara Abbott, Gulf Breeze, FL, took an early retirement from her career as art and English teacher with Shelby County, TN schools to pursue other interests which include photography, painting, cooking, pottery and traveling. She edited *Grandmother Earth's Healthy and Wise Cook Book.*

Jane E. Allen, Wetumpka, AL, enjoys writing fiction, nonfiction, and poetry--and entering contests. Her works have been published in *Progressive Farmer*; *Ordinary and Sacred As Blood: Alabama women speak*; *Grandmother Earth*; *Tough Times, Strong Women*; *The Alalitcom*; *103 Rosie the Riveter Stories*; *Mystery Time; Garden Poems;* and *Cosmic Brownies*. Her children's story, "The Storm Cellar," was recently published by the Chattanooga Writers' Guild. She is a member of Montgomery Branch (AL), NLAPW; Montgomery Press and Authors Club;

Alabama Writers' Conclave; and Women in the Arts (WITA).

Jo Anne Allen recently moved to Grand Junction, CO to be near her three sons. She continues to write, enjoys horseback riding, and spending time with people. She also has a farm in AR where her writing career began.

Annetta Talbot Beauchamp, Helena, AR, is a member of PRA, East Central Branch. She frequently wins regional and national awards.

Edna Carpenter Booker, Iowa City, IA, is a member of the University Club Writers and NLAPW and has published in *Pen Woman, Fairfax Journal, Press Citizen, Cedar Rapids Gazette, Midwest Poetry Review, The Iowa City Gazette Lyrical Iowa*, and numerous State magazines. Her husband was in the Air Force for 28 years They have 3 children, 9 grandchildren, 2 great grandchildren. She won 2 awards in the Life Press National Contest this year.

Von S. Bourland is a Texas poet whose award-winning poems have been published in NFSPS Encore 2003, Golden Words 2003-2004, Poetry Society of Texas Book of the Year 2003, 2004, and 2005, and Mississippi Poetry Journal 2005 and will be published in NFSPS Encore 2005. West Texas cotton farm remembrances and family memories of music and faith influence many of her poems. The vastness of the great plains captures her muse to send her pencil tip-toeing across any scrap of paper close at hand. She served as 1st Vice President of the Hi-Plains Chapter of the Poetry Society of Texas and is President of that organization.

Laurie Boulton, Melbourne, FL, [pen name Lauri Silver] BA, M.Ed.; retired. Published in journals and specialized magazines, *Kicker, Grapevine*; newspapers, *Florida Today*. Won several non-fiction short story/essay awards and numerous poetry awards in many states. Her specialty area is photography to illustrate poems for and about veterans. Two photo illustrated books, for and about veterans (free to veterans) Echoes of the Heart for family and friends.

Florence Bruce, Memphis, TN, a retired medical transcriptionist writes and edits for local physicians. She has won numerous awards including *Grandmother Earth's* top prose award in 1998.

Bill Caudle, Summertown, TN is a Florida Native. He is an attorney [still licensed in Florida] and published author: he has published legal treatises and historical fiction, notably *The Canal* in 1999 and a vignette recently published in *The Irriantum*, a quarterly magazine. Bill and his wife Cheri are writing a musical play entitled *Pennington's Dream*, about Lawrence County's own "Aerial Bird" inventor, James Jackson Pennington, which was produced in 2003, the centennial year of the Wright Brothers' flight at Kitty Hawk, North Carolina.

N. E. Chapman, Oklahoma, City, OK, has, since beginning serious writing twenty years ago, won more than 400 awards in writing contests and has had 100 stories/articles published in local, state, national and international publications. While working as a personnel director for a large hospital, she wrote personnel policies, employee handbooks and a monthly employee newspaper. She has four novels ready for publication.

CJ Clark is from Hardy, AR.

Arla and **John Clemons**, Las Crosse, WI, enjoy proof-reading each other's work. She is a retired physical education teacher, now pursuing her writing career. She has been published in the *Wisconsin Poets' Calendar, Touchstone, Promise Magazine, Grandmother Earth, Julian's Journal* and *Splintered Sunlight* (Anthology 2000 published by the Arizona State Poetry Society). Grandmother of nine, she grew up on a farm, and writes today of those memories. He is a retired physician and has previously published in *Grandmother Earth.*

Sandra Corona, Prineville, OR, has had art work published previously in *Grandmother Earth.*

John Crawford, Professor of English Literature at Henderson State University, Arkadelphia, AR, is also a noted pianist.

Daniel Dahlquist, Galena, Illinois, received his Ph.D. in Speech Communication with an emphasis in Performance Studies from Southern Illinois University. He was Director of Forensics (Competitive Speaking and Interpreting) at the University of Wisconsin-Platteville for 5 years. He currently teaches Interpersonal Communication, Leadership and Communication in Small Groups, and the Public Speaking course in the Long Distance Learning Program at UW-P. Dahlquist studied with James Dickey in the early 1980's, and received a MFA degree from Iowa Writer's Workshop at the University of Iowa in 1984. He has published two books of poetry, *Speech to the Dead People* and *The Highwheel Driver.* In April, 2005, he was one of three Iowa poets chosen to perform at the Des Moines National Poetry Festival with Poet Laureate/Pulitzer Prize winning poets Ted Kooser and Billy Collins. He performs his own work in college and university settings and for a wide range of organizations.

Carl Danna from beautiful Saratoga Springs, NY, is a retired teacher with 10 grandchildren whom he spoils every chance he gets. He's also a sometime stage and screen actor, now appearing in the feature film, *Dorian Blues.*

Michael R. (Mick) Denington, a retired Air Force colonel, writes poetry and fiction. He has won numerous prizes and his works have appeared in local, regional and international publications. He is active in local and state writing organizations, currently serving on the board of the PST. Mick judges poetry contests and has been editor in chief of *Writers on the River* for five years. He and his wife, Marilyn, live in Bartlett, TN.

Frieda Beasley Dorris, Memphis, TN, is one of the originators of the Dorsimbra poetry form. A past president of the Poetry Society of TN, she has won numerous awards for her poetry.

Pat Durmon, a retired mental health counselor, lives in the Ozark Mountains of Arkansas. Poetry and life teach her the same thing: to keep her eyes wide open and to enjoy the journey.

AnneMarie Dyer, Kentucky Colonel, Dunedin, FL, is a private detective. She likes to ride horses and has a dog named Colonel. She is the niece of Cornelius Hogenbirk.

Winifred Hamrick Farrar is Poet Laureate of Mississippi and her work has been widely published. She is a member of the Mississippi Poetry Society, the Poetry Society of Tennessee, and the NLAPW, Chickasaw Branch.

Carol Ogden Floyd, Linton, IN loves animals and nature, reading, playing piano, dulcimer and 10-string harp. She is Indiana State Federation of Poetry Clubs Poet Laureate for 2004-2007.

Lenna Reynolds Frye, a registered nurse and her husband, Merwin, retired from Hutchinson, Kansas to Bella Vista, Arkansas in 2002. Shortly after moving she started drawing and has been encouraged by artists from both Judson Baptist Church and The Village Art Club where she has membership.

Dena R. Gorrell, Edmond, Oklahoma is a widely published writer who often wins national awards. I have been writing poetry since age nine. I am an avid poetry contestant, always keeping something in the mail. Have published four books of poetry including *Truths, Tenderness and Trifles* and *Sunshine and Shadow*. She is often called upon to judge poetry contests at the local, state, and national levels. She wins about 100 awards per year.

Rita Goodgame Little Rock, AR, has been published in *Woman's World, Grandmother Earth, Soiree, Hearts at Home* and a *Fordham Anthology*. She won Arkansas Writers' Grand Conference Literary Award, 2003, and First Place Awards in *Byline Magazine* and The National League of American Pen Women, Pioneer Branch.

Malu Graham, Memphis, TN, won the Hackney Award for fiction (Birmingham Southern College). She has poems and short stories published in *St. Petersburg Times, Emerald*

Coast Review, Octoberfest Mag, Broomstick. She has won prizes in fiction from Florida Writers' Competition and from Life Press.

Bonnie Stucki Gudmundson, Bountiful, Utah**,** is a published author, former Speech-language Pathologist, wife of Dr. Ariel George Gudmundson, mother of six children, grandmother of 26 grandchildren, and great grandmother of three great-grandchildren. Besides having numerous poems published, she has won national and state poetry awards. She has published *Wishing You Christmas* Joy (2002) and *Luck, Pluck and Guided Decisions* (2004).

Sarah Hull Gurley is a member of PST and was born and reared in Louisiana. She has a degree in Business Administration from Louisiana Technical College. Member of St. Luke's United Methodist Church. Currently residing in Germantown, Tennessee and Leesburg, Florida.

Sandra Hancock lives in Benton, TN on the Big Sandy River from which she obtains inspiration for writing. She teaches second grade at Camden Elementary School and belongs to three writers groups.

Verna Lee Hinegardner, Hot Springs, AR, was Poet Laureate of Arkansas for 13 years. She is past president of the AR Pioneer Branch of NLAPW; Past President of PRA; President of Roundtable Poets of Hot Springs; served 12 years on the board of NFSPS and chaired two of their national conventions; member of Poets' Study Club, Poetry Society of America, International Poetry Society, and is listed in The International Directory of Distinguished Leadership. Hinegardner was inducted into the AR Writers' Hall of Fame in 1991; won their Sybil Nash Abrams Award in 1973, 1979 and 1991; and received the AR Award of Merit in 1976 and 1983; and is the author of twelve books of poetry.

William J. Holland, Bastrop, TX, is published widely and has won numerous awards.

Glenna Holloway, Naperville IL,has been published in many magazines and literary journals including *Michigan Quarterly Review, Notre Dame Review, Georgia Review* and won the

Pushcart Prize, 2001 and is working on her first book with a grant from the Illinois Arts Council.

Elizabeth Howard, Crossville, TN, is the author of *Gleaners,* Grandmother Earth 2005 and *Anemones,* Grandmother Earth, 1998. Both contain poetry that has been previously published in journals and anthologies. She is a frequent award-winner.

Carrie Inman, Rogue River, OR, has had poetry and artwork published in various magazines and newspapers. She published a poetry collection, *Writing on Tablets of Water.* Her hobbies are quilting, painting, computer graphic/Desktop publishing, private tutoring, and bird watching.

Faye Williams Jones, North Little Rock, AR is a retired school librarian who received numerous awards during her career. She presented workshops at state, regional, national, and international library and media conferences. Memberships include PRA and River Market Poets Branch. She and her husband, Bob Jones, collaborate to create framed poetry and photography exhibits.

Pat King, Albia, IA, is an active member of half a dozen writing organizations and attends workshops every year at the Iowa Summer Writing Festival. Her prose and poetry have been published in numerous magazines, newspapers, literary journals, and anthologies—*Reminisce, The Rotarian, Lucid Stone, Religion and Public Education, Wind,* and others. She judges national poetry contests, gives poetry readings, and enjoys windsurfing and international travel.

Susan Leeds, Delray Beach, Fl. has won 1st Prize (Haiku) in *Grandmother Earth IX,* Finalist, Robert Penn Warren Awards, 3rd Prize, Vi Bagliore Memorial Award(NLAPW),etc. Publications include: *Midwest Poetry Review, Pegasus, Pen Women Magazine, Lucidity, Sun-Sentinel* newspaper (on-line) ,etc. Member—NLAPW, FLSA.

Anne-Marie Legan, Herrin, IL, received from Cader Publishing, Ltd. the 1998 International Poet Of The Year Chapbook Competition, $5,000 grand prize and publication of *My Soul's On A Journey.* Active in Southern IL Writer's

Guild, she has received many awards and has been published widely, including eight poetry books and three mystery novels, *Tattoo of a Wolf Spider Deadly Case* and her latest mystery novel, *Death Shadow.*

Daniel Leonard has won numerous writing awards, including the 2004 and 2005 Appalachian Writers Association's Playwright of the Year. He is a proud father and grandfather and lives in Oak Ridge, TN with his wife Linda, and their cat, Miss Kitty.

Ellaraine Lockie, Sunnyvale, CA, writes poetry, nonfiction books, magazine articles/columns and children's stories. She is well-published and awards including eight nominations for Pushcart Prizes in poetry. She has 4 published chapbooks: *Midlife Muse*, Poetry Forum; *Crossing the Center Line*, Sweet Annie Press; *Coloring Outside the Lines*, The Plowman Press; *Finishing Lines*, Snark Publishing. She frequently judges poetry contests and teaches a poetry/writing workshops for a variety of groups. Nonfiction books are *All Because of a Button: Folklore, Fact and Fiction,* St. Johann Press; *The Gourmet Paper Maker*, Creative Publishing, and *The Low Lactose Kitchen Companion and Cookbook* forthcoming in 2006.

Angela Logsdon, Memphis, TN is a descendant of the Cherokee/Choctaw nations. She strives to reflect the beauty of her heritage in her writing. Her poetry and photography has been previously published in *Grandmother Earth*. She is a member of PST.

Vera Long, Stillwell Ok, is secretary for Stillwell Writers.

Gloria R. Milbrath, Fort Dodge, IA, is a mother of 5 and a grandmother of 8. She is a "late bloomer," as she's only been writing poems seriously for 5 years. While seeing creative efforts in print is a special thrill, the process of "birthing" a poem is a unique learning experience. And I hope to be learning for a long time to come.

Marjorie and **David Millison,** La Conner, WA, are retired, enjoying their hobbies. David's prime interest is nature photography and her interests have been poetry since high school. Marjorie's poetry was read regularly for 10 years on Seattle radio "Reflections" program. She enjoys entering poetry contests and has received numerous awards and has published in many anthologies and national magazines.

Frances W. Muir, Coral Springs, FL is currently a free-lance writer. Her careers have included teaching, electronics techonology, technical writing, journalism and a stint as a legal secretary.

Rosalyn Ostler, Salt Lake City, UT, has published in *Grandmother Earth, ByLine, Encore, Anthology of New England Writers, Poetry Panorama, Pennsylvania Prize Poems,* etc. She co-authored *By the Throat* and is an officer of the Utah State Poetry Society. She is a grandmother and serves in her church and in Scouting.

June Owens, Zephyrhills, FL, has published many poems and won many prizes. Her first book of poetry, *Tree Line,* published by Prospect Press won the Sparrowgrass Poet of the Year. We just learned that **June died on October 10, 2005.**

LaVonne Schoneman, Seattle, WA, is a former actress. Her husband, children and eight grandchildren also reside in WA. She is author of the popular "How to Cope" series on coping with post-polio, she also writes (and judges) fiction and poetry.

N. Colwell Snell, Native of Wyoming. His poetry has won awards locally and nationally and has been published in several anthologies, including *Byline, Poetry Panorama, Encore, Bay Area Poets Coalition, California Quarterly, Grandmother Earth* and *Anthology Literary Magazine.* Co-author of *By the Throat, Selected Poems*, he has been featured "In the Spotlight" of *Poet's Forum Magazine.* He is the current president of the Utah State Poetry Society and the editor of *Utah Sings, Volume VIII.*

Russell Strauss, Memphis, TN, has won numerous awards in the NFSPS contests as well as many state contests. He is President of PST.

Diane Stefan, wife, mother, and grandmother lives with her husband Joe in their mountain home in the peaceful woods of the Arkansas Ozarks. Faith, family, hippos, history and poetry fill Diane's life.

Brett Taylor, Knoxville, TN, is originally from Wartburg, TN. In addition to *Grandmother Earth*, he has published in *Soul Fountain, The Nocturnal Lyric, South by SouthEast, Raw Nervz Haiku, Haiku Headlines, Persimmon, Modern Haiku, Cicada,* and *Cotyledon.*

Vincent J. Tomeo, Flushing, NY, won honorable mention in the Rainer Maria Rilke International Poetry Competition, 1999. His works appear in anthologies, newspapers, magazines and on the tape, "The Sound of Poetry." He has a publication in Braille, Whispers from the Heart. He presents poetry readings for a variety of organizations in New York.

Phylis Ann Warady's prize-winning short fiction, light verse and essays appear regularly in literary journals and magazines in the USA and Canada. To stave off hunger pangs she writes historical novels set in Regency, England.

Marguerite Thoburn Watkins was born in Nani Tal, India, and attended Woodstock School in the Uttaranchal foothills of the Himalayas. She was the fourth generation of her family to live in India. Her childhood was spent in the mountains and in Jabalpur in Central India except for three years during World War II when she was in the US. She has lived most of her adult life in Lynchburg, VA and has written a memoir available through Xlibris, *TWO TAPROOTS, Growing Up in the Forties in India and America.*

Nancy Watts, Ellicott City, MD is a member of New England Writers Association. Her publications include Kota Press, Small Brushes and a first book of poetry, *Of Ways Of Looking At A Woman*, through Rosecroft Publishing at rosecroftpub@yahoo.com

Carol Clark Williams has won local, state and national awards for her poetry. She teaches poetry workshops and seminars. She has authored two poetry collections: *Stories of the Tribe* and *Music Lessons.*

Kitty Yeager, Arkadelphia, AR, is a member of PRA and PST. A frequent winner of National Poetry Awards, she has published a book of verse, *TRACKS OF A UNICORN.* Her poetry pattern, the *SONAKIT,* is composed of Shakespearean Sonnet and free verse. A three-time winner of the Abrams Award in Arkansas, she won the 2002 Best of Festival Award at the PST Mid-South Poetry Festival.

~~~

STUDENT CONTRIBUTORS

Mila Lauren Brinkley is a 2nd grade student at Bailey Station Elementary, Collierville, TN. Clay and Marina Brinkley are her parents.

Whitney Lauren Brinkley, is in the 11th grade at Hernando (MS) High School and is a member of PST. She has been published in *Grandmother Earth* previously.

Jacob Call is in the 11th grade in Melissa Barry's art class at Cordova (TN) High School. Becky House was his art teacher when he sketched his self-portrait.

Navid and Pijom Nia are students at Cordova (TN) Middle School, Navid's poem was published in *Tennessee Voices* and by the NFSPS in the anthology of student winners. He won 4th honorable mention in the 2005 Manningham Awards.

Celia Snow and **Cameron Hidayat** are 3rd grade students of Mrs. Sarah Hamer at White Station Elementary in Memphis, TN.

Christopher, Grade 6, and **Courtney,** Grade 8, **Watts,** attend Ellicott Mills Middle school, in Ellicott City MD. They have been student winners for 3 years.

GRANDMOTHER EARTH
PUBLICATIONS

Prices quoted include postage and apply only if ordered directly from Grandmother Earth

Abbott, Barbara, *GRANDMOTHER EARTH'S HEALTHY AND WISE COOKBOOK*, 1-884289-13-4. Healthy and easy cooking, but not diet. First layer of fat skimmed from Southern cooking. Optabind binding; $9.

Benedict, Burnette Bolin, *KINSHIP*, 1-884289-08. Lyrical poetry by Knoxville poet. Chapbook, 1995, $5.

Cowden, Frances Brinkley, *VIEW FROM A MISSISSIPPI RIVER COTTON SACK*, 1-884289-03-7. This collection of poetry and short prose emphasizes family values and farm life in Mississippi County, Arkansas and life in Memphis, Tennessee. Cloth, gold imprint, 1993, $12.
TO LOVE A WHALE; 1-884289-06-1. Learn about endangered animals from children and educators. Children's drawings, poetry and prose, PB (Perfect bound) 1995, $6.
BUTTERFLIES AND UNICORNS, ED 4, 1-884289-04-5 (Cowden and Hatchett) Poetry for the young and young-at-heart with notes on teaching creative writing. PB, 1994, $6.

Daniel, Jack, *SOUTHERN RAILWAY- FROM STEVENSON TO MEMPHIS*—1-884289-17-7. 1/2x 11with 400+ photographs, 360 pages, 1996. Daniel is an Alabama native who now lives in Cordova, TN. Documents and other papers with heavy emphasis upon history of Southern Railway and its workers. PB, $39. **Only a few available**
MY RECOLLECTIONS OF CHEROKEE, ALABAMA, 1-884289-25, 8 1/2x11. 300+

photographs of author's family history and life in early Cherokee, 232 pages, PB, 1998, $22.

THOROUGHBREDS OF RAILROADING: YESTERDAY AND TODAY, ISBN 1-884289-26-6 1999, 312 pages, 8 1/2x 11, pictorial history of several railroads. PB, $29.

Hatchett, Eve Braden, *TAKE TIME TO LAUGH*: It's the Music of the Soul. 1- 884289-00-2. Humorous poetry taking off on Eden theme. Chapbook, **very limited edition**, 1993, $9.

Howard, Elizabeth, *ANEMONES*, 1-884289-27-4, Prize-winning poetry, all previously published, East Tennessee (Crossville) poet, introduction by Connie Green, creative writing instructor, U.T. 1998, $9.

GLEANERS, 1-884289-47-9. More excellent previously published and prize-winning poems, 2005, $10

Rice, Clovita, *CRYSTAL and CREATURES,* 1-884289-49-5 A collection of prize-winning and previously published poetry by the editor of Voices International. In 1998 she was inducted into the Arkansas Hall of fame. 2005, $10.

Schirz, Shirley Rounds, *ASHES TO OAK,* 1-884289-07-X Poetry of the lakes region by widely-published Wisconsin author. Grandmother Earth chapbook winner, 1995, $4.

GRANDMOTHER EARTH SERIES: $8 each (multiple copies $6 each, Volumes II and III are $4) Order by Volume number.

GRANDMOTHER EARTH II, III and X feature Tennessee writers. Volume IV features Arkansas Writers. Volume VII features Alabama writers. Volume VIII features Mississippi. Volume IX features Florida writers.

LIFE PRESS PUBLICATIONS

Boren, Blanche S., *THORNS TO VELVET. Devotionals from a Lifetime of Christian Experience*. 1-884289-231, Blanche S. Boren, Kivar 7, gold imprint, cloth, $18.

Cowden, Frances Brinkley, *OUR GOLDEN THREAD*: *Dealing with Grief,* 1-884289-10-x, Ed. Personal testimonies and poetry of 40 contributors from clergy and lay writers who deal with different kinds of grief using personal experiences in their faith journeys. Kivar 7 cloth, gold imprint, 1996, $15.

ANGELS MESSENGERS OF LOVE AND GRACE, 1-884289-18-5. True stories of angel experiences by contributors from all walks of life. 96 pages, perfect bound, 1999, $10.

TOWARD IMAGERY AND FORM: A WRITER'S NOTE-BOOK, 1-8884289-29-0. Loose leaf or coil notebook which contains lessons on strengthening writing skills though poetry and prose lessons. Editing, imagery and poetry forms are stressed. Many forms used are explained. Prize-winning examples by contemporary poets. Lessons were from the first five years of Life Press Writers' Association. $10.

Crow, Geraldine Ketchum, BLOOM WHERE YOU ARE TRANSPLANTED, 1-884289-12-6. A resident of Little Rock, Arkansas, Crow grew up in Hot Springs and tells of life in Perry County where she and her husband farmed for several years. Humorous, inspirational approach about moving from the city to the country. **A few left**, 1996, $10.

Davis, Elaine Nunnally, *MOTHERS OF JESUS: FROM MATTHEW'S GENEALOGY,* 1-884289-05-3. Biography of five women mentioned in Matthew. 344 pp. PB, 1994, $11.

EVES FRUIT, 1-884289-11-8, Defense of Eve and implications for the modern woman. PB, 1995, $10.

PATRONS

John D. McVean, D.D.S.

124 Timber Creek Drive, Memphis, TN 38018

Phone: 901-756-1864

Marina Brinkley—901- 619-4023
Prudential Collins/Maury, Inc., Realtors
**I can help sell your old house
and buy your dream home.**

Memphis Woman's Yellow Pages
BUSINESS LISTINGS
www.memphiswyp.com

The ninth annual
Life Press Christian Writers' Conference
(and national contest) will be held August 5, 2006 in
Cordova, Tennessee. Write P. O. Box 2018 Cordova, TN
38088 for more information or download from
www.grandmotherearth.com. **This conference is of
interest to both beginning and seasoned writers.**

108

MEMORIALS

Jack Daniel
April 11, 1928—August 12, 2005
Author of
Southern Railway: From Stevenson to Memphis
My Recollections of Cherokee, Alabama
Thoroughbreds of Railroading: Yesterday and
Today

Ruth Peal Harrell
July 3, 1918- October 2, 2005
Poet and
Faithful Supporter of Children's Poetry

Cornelius Hogenbirk
September 18, 1917—September 27, 2005
Faithful Contributor to Grandmother Earth

Joseph Benton Ray
January 2, 1918—November 30, 2003
Loving Husband
of Lucile Roberts Ray

In Memory of Sam Sax

April 29, 1942—July 1, 2004

By Barbara Britton Abbott

INDEX

Students:

Special Features: